Presented to me, in person, by
Tony Hullis, at "The Top of Toronto"
(the revolving restaurant, CN Tower) —
June 4, 1990.

sale

no

sale $~~500~~

um

final sale
$ 2^{50}
Bm

*By the same author:—*

Southgate — A Glimpse into the Past.
Once Upon a Time in Palmers Green.

*Best wishes*

# Fond Memories
## of
# Winchmore Hill

by
Alan Dumayne

*Alan Dumayne*

First Edition 1990
ISBN 0-9512286-2-5
© 1990 Alan Dumayne
Printed and bound in England by
Macdermott & Chant Ltd.
London and Welshpool

*in dear memory
of my parents*

# CONTENTS

# FOREWORD

AS A BEING of like mind to Alan, borne out by discussions on our early environment and local beginnings, I was honoured when he asked me to contribute the Foreword to this, his latest book on local history, the Winchmore Hill area of the old Borough of Southgate.

I was born here in the early part of the 1914-18 war into a family which had arrived in the locality in the late 1860's and, like Alan, grew to know and love the area. His descriptions of so many of the old landmarks and people have brought back nostalgic memories of childhood, and of talks with my parents and grandparents, on the past.

The sort of people who inhabited the area, and their places of living and working, are vividly portrayed in this gem of a book.

Here we had a heritage carefully and jealously guarded by John Donnithorne Taylor and others, and preserved, sometimes against opposition, by the far-seeing councillors of the past.

Sadly, much has been eroded by those who do not see conservation in the same vein and, but for these books and pictures, would be lost, never to be revealed to the present generation.

The author, I know, greatly deplores these losses, particularly the open spaces, and I am greatly indebted to him for seeing fit to cover the 'Old Borough' with his three books which record so much for posterity, and for the many pictures.

This latest work, which is so worthwhile reading, completes the series, at any rate for the time being – but well, who knows?

Keith Surtees

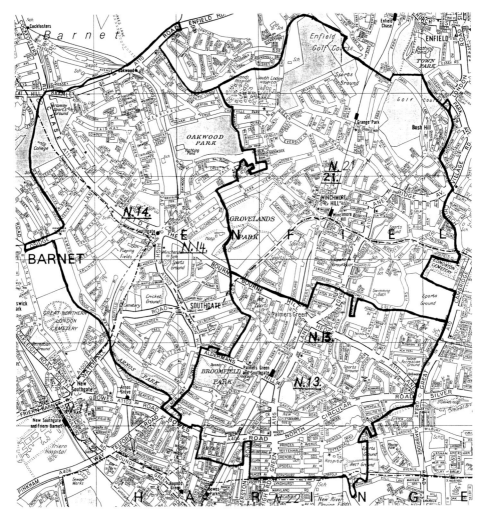

The N13, N14 and N21 districts combine to form an almost circular region, so rich in local history.

# INTRODUCTION

I OWE A GREAT debt to my readers. I cannot pretend that the thought of writing another book on local history (my third) did not fill me with a great deal of apprehension and foreboding. Could I possibly rise to the task? Would the mental cogs turn sufficiently to enable my pencil to move across the lines, without a hint of senility being apparent? Could I summon the energy and drive necessary to carry out my researches, and was I being fair in remaining closeted in my study for hours on end, neglecting other tasks, with only the sound of pencil on paper disturbing the peace? I was already very busy lecturing to many of our local societies on the subject I love, and spending a lot of time in distributing my books on Southgate and Palmers Green to the various outlets. Writing another book would, I knew, make even greater inroads into my time.

With encouragement from all sides, I decided to make a start. That was a big step. Many people have asked me what is the most difficult aspect in writing a book. 'Making a start' comes immediately to mind for, once you have made that initial move, you engage into gear and then hope to keep the motor running.

I have never known time pass so quickly as when I am engaged on these projects. I am sure other authors will confirm. Somehow, when one is immersed in thought and concentration, and the pencil stutters spasmodically into action, the hands of the clock whizz round at twice the normal rate. One may be deep in research surrounded by papers, books, documents and maps in apparent total disarray. One may be meeting people with stories to tell, or just exploring an area that we thought we knew so well, yet is always open to new discovery. The time evaporates and soon we are forced to set aside our research, our thoughts and our pencil for another day.

My enthusiasm remained undimmed, for the story was about my home town where I was raised as a boy and where the memories I have are all good ones. It has not always been easy. Writing, I find, is a lonely occupation. You alone are in control and can gain little help from others, save their unspoken understanding and cooperation. My wife has helped enormously in this respect and the family have long accepted, in the nicest possible way, that Dad is a bit eccentric and past redemption. I am so grateful.

But I come back to you, my readers. It is your response that has kept me going. The encouraging comments, letters and 'phone calls about my previous attempts, have been a revelation to me. At the end of the day the message has been:— 'more power to your elbow', 'keep going old boy', or 'when's the next book coming out?' Should I ever have had any moments of doubt, it is that response and those feelings that would always keep me going. I have endeavoured to reply to all who have responded with such kindness. I say again, thank you for your support and interest.

Winchmore Hill is a very special place to me. I was born in Harringay in 1929 and my parents moved to Winchmore Hill in 1933, when I was 4 years old. I have only to go past 83 Farm Road today and the memories come flooding back. The summerhouse Dad built in the back garden and the air raid shelter we used in the blitz. The chickens we kept to help out the rations, our concerted efforts at 'Dig for Victory', and the birthday parties, when my friends came round to tea.

I can see all the neighbours' faces, though they have long since gone. I always knew them as Mr. or Mrs. So and So, for Christian names were seldom used, certainly as far as adults were concerned. Even close friends of my parents were addressed formally and, likewise, they were known as Mr. and Mrs. Dumayne, seldom as Jack and Ruby. It was the fashion to be formal in those days. I recall, even at school, only our very close chums would be on Christian name terms.

I remember the hours I spent playing football in the road. The garage gates that were the 'goal' are still there. There was Norman, Harold, George and Robin, who would join with me and fashion their incredible skills in dribbling, shooting and ball control, by dint of hours of practice.

I have a mental picture of my Mum and Dad, perpetually young and full of energy. I recall the letters home from brother Ron, serving in India, and sister Pat's first try on the garden swing. Magical moments indeed!

I must not wander from my brief. Were there any special problems with Winchmore Hill? One of the first tasks any author faces is to formulate the chapter headings. As you know, I like to take you, my readers, and also my audiences at my slide shows, on a journey. This proved to be a little more difficult with Winchmore Hill than either Southgate or Palmers Green, but I hope I have reached a satisfactory compromise. Much of the old village, certainly, was centred around the Green with the roads radiating off this focal point, the definitive hub, to all points of the compass. You will appreciate, therefore, the difficulty in devising a journey.

Nevertheless, I have tried to maintain a logical sequence and all will be revealed as the book unfolds.

I have once again used the postal district, N21 in this case, to draw the boundaries of our village. As you will see from the map, the three districts of Southgate, Palmers Green and Winchmore Hill combine quite neatly into a roughly circular region, all suburbia now but once, not very long ago, so very different. Streets and housing now cover the ground, where once were green fields with wooded hills and sheltered valleys. There were brooks and streams that flowed gently through rich farmland. The landed gentry, attracted to the area by its great natural beauty and charm, had built their mansions and private estates here. It was in this setting that our little hamlets were established and grew up. London must have seemed a thousand miles away.

I start by giving a general picture, attempting to stand back and view things from a distance. It is all very well to get close up and go into great detail, but we must pause awhile and see how the pieces fit into the whole.

We examine some of the theories put forward concerning the origin of the name of our village. We discuss Enfield Chase which I describe as 'the jewel of the whole area'. The milestones of events of more recent times are recorded, with particular reference to transport and communication which are vital factors in the development of any region.

The journey starts with a look at the Taylor Walker connection. Here, we can see the great influence these families had on the way in which the area developed. The Taylors, in particular, held the key as far as Winchmore Hill was concerned. The sale of their estates, in 1902, was a turning point about which I have written at length. We recapture the era when the Winchmore Hill Woods were a magical and mysterious playground, and the charcoal burners built their clamps in the forest. Let us go over the stile in Dog & Duck Lane, and along the footpath towards the village, long before Broad Walk was even dreamed of.

We continue with an exploration of the Green, the village centre I call it. We then widen our scope over a considerable radius, including all those roads that lead uphill to the Kings Head, the old village inn, and eventually feed into the Green. My interpretation is broad and gives me licence to include those places and people I find of special interest. This includes the history of our churches, always at the heart of, and playing a vital part in the growth of any village.

I should make reference here to the Paulin and Mann families.

Their influence on the local scene cannot be over-emphasised, as will be made apparent as the story unfolds. It is an extraordinary coincidence that these two great families were in many ways a parallel to the Taylor Walker combination for they, too, were related by marriage with their wealth based on the family brewing business. The Paulins, especially, were generous and caring benefactors to the whole community. The effects are still felt, long after their passing.

The arrival of the railway, in 1871, was a landmark in the life of the village, and I found this period so closely allied to the Cresswell family that I have included both subjects in Chapter 5. It was a fascinating time in our history, for it brought communication to a village that refused to wake from its slumbers, with or without the trains. The wall had been breached, however, and slowly the village that the Cresswells knew so well was to undergo change. The opening of Grange Park station heralded a new area of development. Gradually the big houses and the farmsteads disappeared from view.

The Green Lanes is now one of the main arteries in North London, but it was not always so. It brought late development to Winchmore Hill on its eastern side, but only after the turn of the century as we shall discover in Chapter 6. We commence our journey at the Methodist Church opposite Barrowell Green, and head northwards. We learn more about Highfield House and its park, only a fragment of which remains. We rediscover Fords Grove, the mansion which once stood on the site of the old Capitol cinema, now just a memory. And so we continue past the lovely Beaulieu estate and the Green Dragon up to Masons Corner, with so much of our history to discover along the way.

Bush Hill followed in logical sequence for it was once called Green Lanes and continued the journey northwards to the limit of our region. The reasons for the diversion of the main road, and the effect this had, are discussed in Chapter 7. Bush Hill and the New River are always linked together in my mind because Sir Hugh Myddleton, prime motivator of the project, lived at Bush Hill House, and it was in his grounds that the great aqueduct was constructed. Accordingly, I have combined these subjects. I have long been interested in the New River and never cease to marvel at the ingenuity of its construction, way back in 1609-13.

As we approach the Enfield borders we have another look at the once vast Old Park estate and at Bush Hill Park, the large mansion set in beautiful grounds that has long since disappeared from sight.

I have great personal affection for the eastern side of our region where I spent my boyhood years. I hope this comes across in Chapter 8, which I call Firs Lane and Around. There are many stories to unfold concerning Barrowell Green, Firs Lane, Farm Road, Highfield Road and Fords Grove, with special reference to the Winchmore Hill Cricket Club and the Paulins.

I close with a few personal memories in Chapter 9. These memories are not, in themselves, important or particularly significant but I find that very often they spark off a host of recollections from my readers. Their memories, indeed *your* memories, hitherto locked away, are given a key whereby they are released again, as your past is recalled and the mental pictures of days gone by sharpen into focus. If I have been able to stimulate such thoughts, I shall be pleased.

This is not a definitive history of Winchmore Hill. To cover this ground in its entirety would require several volumes. That was never my intention. In the final analysis, I have felt the need to edit, rather than expand. For all my omissions, I offer my sincere apologies. I have tried to be accurate by checking and rechecking my facts but, in such a story, I may well have erred. I have usually indicated where the tales are merely legendary with little or no substantiation, so you may accept them for what they are worth. I regret my many shortcomings in a book that has involved a lot of hard work and countless hours of dedication, but which has given me a great deal of pleasure. I hope it has proved worthwhile.

Is Winchmore Hill really a lost village, when we can recall so many treasured moments? There are still many good things that remain. Let us try to keep them. Where we have to change, let us consider the long term effect on our environment, not only the short term expediency. There have been many far-sighted people in the past, to whom we owe so much for their wise counsel and guidance. Let us not betray them now, as we look towards the future.

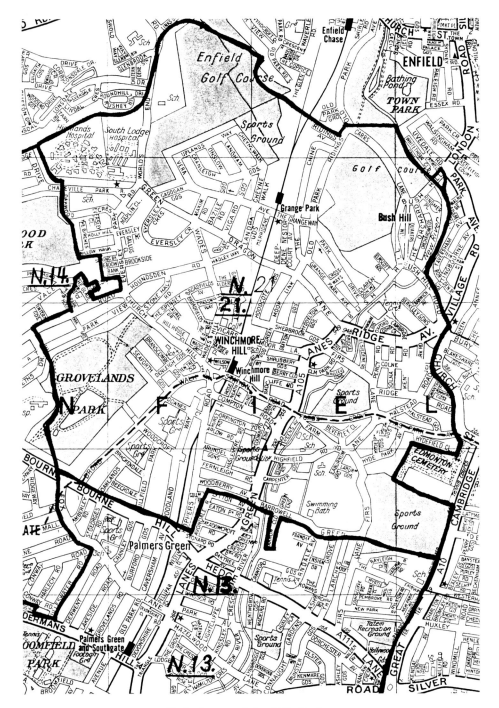

Today's map of the N21 district.

# CHAPTER 1

## THE GENERAL PICTURE

THE ORIGIN OF the name Winchmore Hill has confounded the historians and the researchers over the years, for there are different theories put forward, none of which may be correct.

With the experts divided on such matters, as in the case of Palmers Green, one treads on dangerous ground reaching one's own conclusions for, whatever they may be, it will not satisfy all parties. Over the years, as with the name of Palmers Green, the subject has cropped up, from time to time, in the columns of our local newspapers with a spate of letters from correspondents, each one convinced that *their* theory *must* be the correct one. I can only summarise.

In the 17th century, a well was sunk by a vicar of Edmonton, to provide water for his parishioners on the moor, Winchmore Hill being at the time within the parish of Edmonton. The well was situated in what came to be known as Vicars Moor Lane. It appears that, originally, the well was fitted with a winch and windlass, though latterly the water level was high enough for it to be used as a 'dipping' well. In the past, many have contended that these circumstances gave birth to the name of our village, i.e. the *winch* of the well, combined with the *moor* at the top of the *hill*. This has long since been ridiculed by the antiquarians, for the basic roots of the name had been formulated some 300 years before the well was sunk.

In fact, the earliest reference to Winchmore Hill is in a deed dated 1319AD where the name is spelt Wynsemerhull and, in 1543 and 1565, documents clearly refer to Wynsmore Hill. The reference books on place names (Oxford & Gover's) reason thus. They say it is probably derived from the old English 'Wynsige' (a person's name) and 'maerhyll' (a boundary hill), i.e. the hill at the boundary of Wynsige's land.

Henrietta Cresswell, as she makes clear in her book, favoured yet another theory. She thinks it likely to have been derived from the moor at the top of the hill, on which the whin (or furze) grew plentifully, the Whinsmoor Hill. Miss Cresswell's may be the less authoritative voice in the argument, but I do not readily discount her theory. She was a highly intelligent woman, who would only have formed an opinion after the most careful thought and study, before drawing her own conclusions. Also, she was born in the village and grew up here with her parents, both of whom had lived the major part of their lives in the district. Such knowledge is often

1

handed down through the many generations of the local families living in the village. These are people to whom Miss Cresswell, and the doctor and his wife, would have had ready access.

Usually known for his accuracy and detailed research, Colonel Arthur Willis, under his pen name Memorabilia, seemed to favour the whin (or furze) on the moor theory. He attended a lecture in 1901, given by the Winchmore Hill Literary Society, on the subject. The speaker maintained that the hamlet of Winchmore Hill had its origin in pre-Tudor days, when a small body of people suffering religious persecution took refuge among the huge and high whin bushes, which covered the site of the Green and much of the surrounding land. The whin was said to be so dense that it was almost inpenetrable. There, the refugees made a small clearing and built primitive shelters, which in course of time developed into a few small cottages, the hamlet and the village. Fact or fiction, history or legend? I suppose we shall never know.

It would be interesting to discover if Winchmore Hill in Buckinghamshire, south west of Amersham, has any historical background to its name.

In giving the general background to our area I do ask forgiveness for any repetition of matters discussed in my previous books, but it is unavoidable.

In early times a huge forest, the great Middlesex forest, had covered a vast expanse to the north of London. Gradually, inroads and clearings were made and small settlements and farms became established. Tracks were cut to maintain some lines of communication, enabling the farmer to buy and sell his livestock and market his produce.

We must not forget the jewel of the whole area, Enfield Chase. Back in the mists of time, before the Conquest, Enfield Chase was part of a much larger estate thought to be in the hands of Asgar, who became Master of the Horse and Constable of the Army. William the Conqueror was a great believer in rewarding his loyal supporters by the distribution of land, and it was by this means that Geoffrey de Mandeville, a powerful Norman baron, acquired this area as part of the Manor of Enfield.

By inheritance, the Chase was handed down through generations of the Mandeville and De Bohun families until, on the death of Joan de Bohun in 1419, the manor passed into the hands of Henry V. His father (Henry IV), when he had been the Earl of Derby, had married Mary, the younger daughter and co-heir of the late Humphrey de Bohun. The final partition of the estates took place in

2

1421, when Enfield Manor and Chase was allocated to the King as part of the Duchy of Lancaster. It was to remain in Royal hands for more than 350 years.

Those who owned land adjoining the Chase were duty bound to hedge, fence or ditch the perimeter to prevent the game escaping. Above all, the deer was the sacred animal to be preserved, if only to provide quarry for the Royal hunting parties. The penalties for unlawful killing and poaching of game were very severe indeed.

The villagers enjoyed certain rights and privileges on Enfield Chase, though they were controlled and sometimes restricted. As commoners, their sheep and cattle would be allowed to graze there. Pigs could be fattened on the acorns and the beechmast in the autumn. They had certain rights in coppicing parts of the forest and in the gathering of kindling wood, to provide fuel for their hearths and for their cooking.

The south eastern boundary of the Chase, in our N21 area, ran along Winchmore Hill Road (once called Chase Side for obvious reasons) and continued to meet what is now Green Dragon Lane, where it joined with the boundary of Old Park. We can see, therefore, that the area of the Chase within our district was much less than in the case of Southgate, but we have to think in broader terms when assessing its influence on the character of the whole region.

Enfield Chase extended northwards as far as Potters Bar and totalled 8,351 acres prior to disafforestation* in 1777. Winchmore Hill, at the time, was part of the Edmonton parish, the freeholders of which were allocated land totalling 1,231 acres to compensate for their rights and privileges, lost by the division of the Chase. It all took time and the nineteenth century had begun before the Commissioners had set their seals on the final documents.

And so the life of Enfield Chase grew slowly to a close.

Our area was one of great natural beauty and, as the tiny hamlets grew, some wealthy and titled families were attracted and encouraged to build their mansions and create their great estates in our midst. The policies of these great landowners, the Taylors in particular, are discussed in the next chapter, so I shall not elaborate. Briefly, they did all in their power to maintain the status quo and prevent any development taking place.

One of the key factors was transportation, or the lack of it. True,

*disafforest – to free from the operation of forest laws;
              to reduce from the legal state of forest
              to that of ordinary land.

3

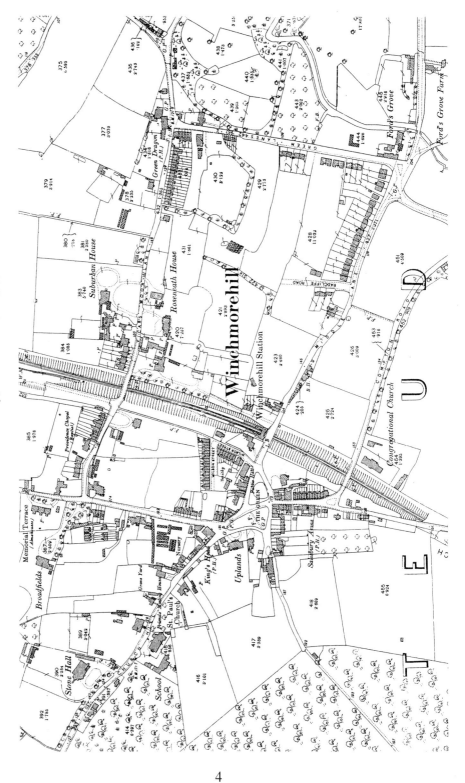

Ordnance Survey, Second Edition 1897.

4

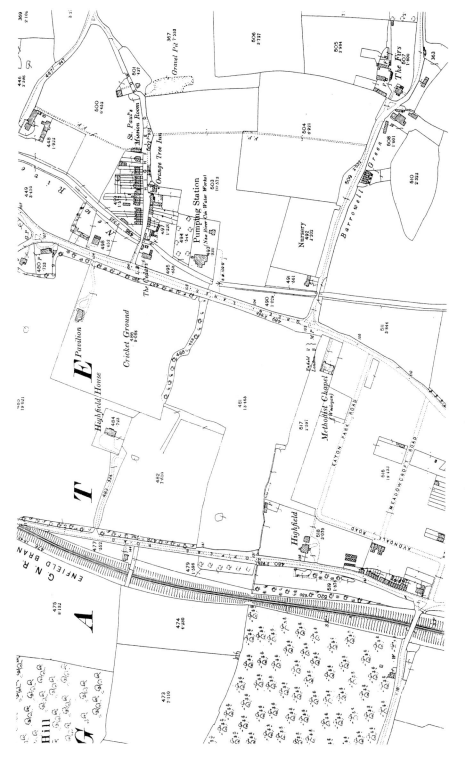

We can learn so much about the past by studying old maps.

5

in spite of Mr. Taylor's opposition, the railway did arrive in Winchmore Hill in 1871, but the effect was far less dramatic than it proved further to the east. Here, with the rail link established between Lower Edmonton and Liverpool Street, the Great Eastern Railway offered cheap workmen's returns (twopence) into town and back. It had an immediate effect and led to a rapid alteration in the nature of Edmonton and Tottenham. Within a few years, the building of artisan houses accelerated and the big red brick Georgian houses disappeared. What had been high class residential districts became working class areas. Meanwhile, the western half of the parish (Southgate, Palmers Green and Winchmore Hill) remained a rural backwater of big estates, farms and middle class villas.

Perhaps I should outline a few of the more important milestones. Having been under the control of its eastern neighbour for more than 500 years, Southgate (including Palmers Green and Winchmore Hill) separated from Edmonton in 1881. The reasons for this and the efforts of Sir Ralph Littler, the last tenant of Broomfield House who set up the separatist movement, have been fully discussed in my previous books. It was a very important turning point.

The Southgate Local Board of Health was established, with their offices at Ash Lodge, near the Cherry Tree. Southgate became an Urban District in 1894 and steadily grew in importance. This was duly recognised in 1933, when the Charter of Incorporation was presented by HRH the Prince George (later to become the Duke of Kent) and Southgate became a Municipal Borough, totalling 3,765 acres. The population in 1881 was 8,289 people, living in 1,694 homes. Fifty years later this had climbed to 55,570 people, living in 14,750 homes, and the numbers were still rising.

The 1930's were, I suppose, the halcyon days when Winchmore Hill was proud to be part of what came to be known as 'the Queen of the Boroughs'.

In 1965, under the London Government Act of 1963, Southgate came under the control of the London Borough of Enfield. Along with many other boroughs, it then lost its independence and became a small part of an even larger authority than the one it had fought to leave in 1881. The wheel had turned full circle.

I have already mentioned the important factor of transport and accessibility. For centuries it was the horse that provided man with his greatest ally in the quest for travel. A man on horseback still gives me this wonderful vision of an inseparable team with the power, the freedom and the ability to roam unconfined to the ends of the world. The trusty steed could be relied on, come what may, to obey his master's will and carry him safely and speedily to his required destination. I must be influenced still by all those Westerns I saw at the cinema in my youth.

As the paths became tracks, that developed into roads, there followed the attachment of all sorts of carts, gigs and carriages of many shapes, sizes and varieties for the horse (or team of horses) to pull us along.

The horsebus, one of the first public conveyances on our roads, duly arrived. In the early days, the control of these was usually in the hands of the landlords of the local inns, and Winchmore Hill was no exception. After all, the inns usually possessed suitable stabling facilities, and could provide refreshment and accommodation for the traveller, if needed, at the end of his journey. All my books make reference to this typical part of our local scene, which only faded from view during the early years of this century.

The railway arrived in Winchmore Hill in 1871 and prompted a gradual change. Although some horsebus services still ran their long journeys into town and back, they came to be used more and more as a shuttle service taking passengers to and from the local railway station. Here, they could catch their morning train into town, and then be met in the evening for the final stage of their journey home. The first of the commuters!

Then came the motor car. Need I say more? The first one appeared in our area in 1901. It was owned by Doctor A.S. Ransome, who lived for some years at The Lawns in Crown Lane, Southgate and whose practice was on the corner of Broomfield Lane and Green Lanes in Palmers Green. It was a 3½ h.p. Benz with a cruising speed of about 12 m.p.h., with solid tyres. The wheels at the front were much smaller than those at the rear. Anyone could drive the vehicle, unlicensed and without number plates, in those days. What would the doctor make of today's cars and the congestion on our roads?

Of all the changes in our environment since the turn of the century, and there have been many, I count the tremendous growth in traffic, both on our roads and in the skies, as the most significant and far-reaching of all.

The invention of the internal combustion engine heralded the subsequent arrival of the motor buses, which reached Southgate in 1912. The London General Omnibus Company was established, followed by a host of independent 'pirate' bus operators.

Far more significant to Winchmore Hill, however, was the arrival of the trams. The major undertaking of extending the electric tramway northwards from Manor House, along the Green Lanes as far as Winchmore Hill, was completed by the autumn of 1907. Initially, the trams only went as far as the Green Dragon but, by 1909, the service had been extended to Enfield.

This established the Green Lanes, once and for all, as a major route into and out of London, and led to development along its road frontages. Gradually, the Green Lanes was ceasing to live up to its name. The original village of Winchmore Hill around the Green, and its railway station nearby, had been established to the west of this now important highway and a secondary 'village', albeit a modern one, grew up with shops along the Broadway, many of which were built in 1904-5 in anticipation of the arrival of the trams, a few years later.

These shops were to serve a growing community on the eastern side of the region, and subsequent developments at the Green Dragon and at Masons Corner were just part of the process of Winchmore Hill developing from a village into a more scattered suburb of a growing metropolis.

The ominous signs had already appeared with the break-up of the Bowes Manor estate in 1899. The sale of the Taylor estates in 1902 was a major landmark which heralded a new era in the structure of our society, indeed in life itself, within the confines of our region. The next thirty years or so were to see the break-up of all the big estates and the farmsteads, the disappearance of many of the large houses and their grounds, the development of roads, shops and housing over a wide area, and the change from village life to suburbia.

The auctioneers and the estate agents, the civil engineers and the authorities, the architects and the builders – all played their parts in this transformation. Those who lived through it speak of an experience they will never forget, for it all happened so quickly that the scene had changed, even before they realised it.

The extension of the Piccadilly Line from Wood Green, out to Cockfosters, in 1933, was to have an immediate effect on house building in neighbouring areas such as Oakwood, Southgate and Arnos Grove. Gradually, the joining up process continued, as suburb linked to suburb, and the open spaces grew fewer and fewer. The brake had been released and there was no turning back. 1938 saw the end of the trams in our locality and the introduction of the trolleybuses. With the outbreak of war, in September 1939, we had come to the end of another chapter.

# CHAPTER 2
## THE TAYLOR WALKER CONNECTION

TO BE TRUTHFUL, I was in a great quandary introducing my next character on these pages, i.e. Mr. John Donnithorne Taylor, about whom I have already written at length in my Southgate and Palmers Green books. My first inclination was to pass him over, knowing that many of you will have learnt of him from my previous writings. On reflection, however, I realised that this would be foolish for he was a vital character, who played a crucial part in the story of Winchmore Hill. To write any sort of history of the area without expanding on 'JDT', would be like recording the history of World War II without mentioning Sir Winston Churchill.

Taylor played such an important role in how the whole area was to develop, and at what pace it was to be allowed to develop, that it is essential to include his story in these pages. His influence was so far-reaching as to affect not only Southgate, Palmers Green and Winchmore Hill, but also many areas beyond these boundaries. I do, however, apologise to my readers for such repetition. Each book has its own separate story to tell and must stand on its own. Inevitably there is some unavoidable overlapping.

The next few pages contain much already written in my Southgate book about the man, his mansion and the estate on which he lived. All three, in a way, are inseparable. I have altered the text here and there and expanded where necessary to emphasise his influence on the Winchmore Hill area, the village and its people. At the time of his death, his estates totalled nearly 600 acres, about half of which lay in what is now the N21 district.

At the junction of Queen Elizabeth Drive and The Bourne, on the north-eastern corner, is a lodge and an entrance to the house we know as Grovelands. Reference to the map will indicate that Taylor's old home (Grovelands) and the immediate grounds are in the Southgate, N14 area but the bulk of the Grovelands Estate, some 300 acres stretching as far east as Hoppers Road, is in the Winchmore Hill, N21 area.

There is so much to tell it is difficult to know where to start. The land, originally part of the great Middlesex forest and densely wooded, had once been owned by Lord Burghley, when it was known as Lords Grove.

Mr. Walker Gray had the house built in 1797-8 and changed the name to Southgate Grove. The combination of John Nash (architect) and Humphry Repton (landscape gardener) gave birth to the beauty, some of which is still evident today. Mr. Walker Gray, brewer by trade, must have been wealthy and influential to employ men of such calibre. His father was Mr. Abraham Gray of Tottenham and his mother Henrietta, sister of the first Isaac Walker who had lived at Southgate House before buying Arnos Grove.

Round about 1835, John Donnithorne Taylor bought the house and the estate following the death of his uncle, Walker Gray, all of 230 acres, and his policy was soon apparent. At every opportunity 'JDT', as he is often referred to, continued to buy up land.

His father, John Vickris Taylor, who died in 1828, had lived in Fox Lane in a house, roughly where Selborne Road enters today.

Initially, 'JDT' changed the name of his house and immediate estate to Woodlands, but soon relented and called it Grovelands, as it remains to this day. He died at Grovelands on 13th December 1885, aged 87.

What of these 50 years that 'JDT' lived here? Why did he continue to buy up land with such insatiable appetite? Just what influence did he have on the area and its surroundings? I hope the answers to these questions will unfold in due course.

Firstly, a word about the connections with Taylor Walker, the brewers of Limehouse. The Brewery was built and the Company of Harford & Taylor was founded in 1730; in 1816, Isaac Walker joined and the name was changed to Taylor Walker; in 1827, John Donnithorne Taylor became a partner in the firm (succeeding his father and grandfather before him); in 1843, the Taylors sold out to Isaac and Edwin Walker and the Walkers, then, were in sole control.

Thereafter, the control of the Company passed down the family until V.E. Walker took charge. He was one of the last generation of Walkers and, when he died in 1906, his nephew John Bradshaw took over as President and Chairman, until his death in 1939.

As we can see, Taylor Walker was very much an inter-related partnership of two great families, with all concerned having strong local connections. Their names will forever be entwined, not only for their business and family connections, but also for their policies and attitudes as landowners in our midst.

Picture the scene. Southgate was an area of great beauty. Enfield Chase had been disafforested in 1777 but had remained unspoilt for many years, a lasting fragment of the great Middlesex forest. The wooded countryside, with its green hills and valleys, was still a peaceful haven. The small villages of Southgate, Palmers Green and Winchmore Hill were still quite isolated. In between were the farms and the estates of those attracted to the area, the wealthy landowners. They liked what they saw and they wanted to keep it that way.

London was expanding and the pressure was on for more roads, more houses, more development. Some landowners reacted by buying up more land. In this way, they had more control over their environment.

Their road frontages remained undeveloped; the estate and property developers were scorned; road and railway development was strongly resisted. With transport, communication and access denied, the area could not develop. It has been aptly described as a 'private green belt policy' and it succeeded – for a time.

The Walkers and others assisted, but by far the chief advocate of these policies, certainly as far as this area was concerned, was John Donnithorne Taylor.

In spite of his opposition, the Great Northern Railway constructed a branch line in 1871, through Palmers Green and Winchmore Hill out to Enfield, but development remained in very low key.

Following JDT's death in 1885, his son Robert Kirkpatrick Taylor took control of the estates until his death in 1901 when his son, Captain John Vickris Taylor of the Welsh Guards (JDT's grandson) took over.

The writing was on the wall. Surrounding districts had already yielded to the developers. The tide could not be stemmed indefinitely. Captain Taylor was planning to marry and move out to Oxfordshire.

On 9th June 1902, the Taylor estates in their entirety were put on the market. The newspaper headline 'Southgate For Sale' was not unduly exaggerated. The sale consisted of 13 separate lots, over a very wide area, affecting Southgate, Palmers Green and Winchmore Hill. I think it is worthwhile listing them.

LOT 1.     The 'Old Park' estate, about 130 acres, between Aldermans Hill and Fox Lane with frontages to Fox Lane, Aldermans Hill, Cannon Hill & High Street. Bought by the British Land Company for £45,000.

LOT 2.     The Fox P.H., about 1½ acres. Bought by Huggins & Co (Brewers) for £11,020.

LOT 3.     About 9 acres south of The Fox, with valuable frontage on to Green Lanes. Bought for £10,150.

LOT 4.     S.W. Corner of the Triangle junction, valuable frontage to the Triangle, Green Lanes and Aldermans

|          |                                                                                                                    |
|----------|--------------------------------------------------------------------------------------------------------------------|
|          | Hill, about ¾ acre. Bought by Mr. Sinclair for £2,200.                                                              |
| LOT 5.   | Plot between Aldermans Hill and Broomfield Lane, about 2 acres. Bought by Councillor Peek for £555.                 |
| LOT 6.   | Plot between Aldermans Hill and Broomfield Lane, west of the railway line, about 5 acres. Bought for £4,050.        |
| LOT 7.   | The Hermitage residence in Cannon Hill with 1¼ acres and 100 ft. frontage. Not sold.                               |
| LOT 8.   | 'Cannon Hill' with 3 acres and 370 ft. frontage. Not sold.                                                         |
| LOT 9.   | The Grovelands estate extending to Winchmore Hill Road in the N.W., Church Hill in the N.E., Bourne Hill in the S.W., Railway in the E. 314 acres. Not sold. |
| LOT 10.  | Home Farm (Kings Farm) Estate 62 acres. Bought for £8,400.                                                          |
| LOT 11.  | Strip of land between Hoppers Road and railway, 2½ acres. Bought by Mr. Berry for £2,100.                           |
| LOT 12.  | The Lodge Estate in Palmers Green. 27 acres. Not sold.                                                              |
| LOT 13.  | The Waterfall Estate. 24 acres. Bought for £5,500.                                                                  |

June 9th, 1902 was a momentous day. It was the day the Taylor estates went up for sale. It was the watershed when the course was changed forever and there was to be no going back. The march of time would not be delayed any longer. That much revered local historian, Tom Mason, described it as 'the pistol shot' that rang out to signal the end of village life. This was certainly true as far as Palmers Green was concerned. Perhaps the effect was less immediate and less dramatic in Southgate and Winchmore Hill.

What would 'JDT' have thought about it all? Not much I fear. It is difficult to glean much of his character from the old records. He was a man of very strong personality and convictions, without the popular appeal of the Walker brothers. However, *they* were sportsmen and the villagers could more easily identify with men they could see regularly exercising their skills in Southgate's favourite sport. There was communication with the Walkers, both on and off the field.

Not so with 'JDT'. He married Elizabeth Henrietta Thompson in 1830 and, as far as we know, was a good father to his children and master to his staff. His two interests, according to Herbert Newby, were hunting and the acquisition of land. He could often be seen in his latter years, working on his estate, doing quite menial tasks,

*(left)*
John Donnithorne Taylor of Grovelands, taken in the Birdcage Room in 1880.

*(below)*
Grovelands. Let us be thankful that the house still serves a useful purpose and has been preserved for future generations.

The footpath through Winchmore Hill Woods, taken in 1884, which has
become Broad Walk today.

dressed in a countryman's smock, and looking more like a farm hand, instead of the great landowner that he was.

He was buried on 18th December 1885. On his instructions, there was no mourning. The coffin was taken by eight bearers on a four-wheeled bier from the house, around his beloved lake, across Bourne Hill by the Woodman, down the footpath (now called The Mall) through two clap-gates, past the Cherry Tree and across the Green to Christ Church. There, in the Church graveyard, he was buried. A large flat stone covers the vault with the only inscription 'JDT'.

The parts of the Taylor estates that came within the boundaries of Winchmore Hill included the bulk of Lot No. 9, the Grovelands Estate, and Lot No. 11, the strip of land between Hoppers Road and the railway. The bidding for Lot No. 9 did not reach the reserve price and was withdrawn from sale. I doubt if it was realised at the time what a blessing this was. The land could so easily have fallen prey to the developers. In no time at all the whole area would have been covered with roads and housing. As it was, the Grovelands estate remained in the hands of the trustees with its future in abeyance.

Captain Taylor was duly married in 1903, and there are photographs of him and his wife returning to Grovelands from honeymoon and being greeted by his staff on arrival. The happy couple decided not to move out straight away. There were, after all, important estate matters still to be settled, particularly regarding those lots remaining unsold, Nos. 7, 8, 9, and 12, the most important by far being the family home and its grounds of 314 acres.

It seemed a wise move for the Captain and his wife to be on hand, and a vital one as far as Winchmore Hill was concerned. Whilst the Taylors were still in residence, they exercised control and could respond to local interests. The trustees may well have been tempted otherwise. The Captain had been steeped in his grandfather's policies, and knew how hard and how long 'JDT' had fought to preserve the beauty of the area. He could not lightly throw it all away.

A consortium had ambitious plans to purchase the whole estate and build a 'Woodlands City' that would be a showpiece for the rest of the world. There would be wide boulevards and luxury homes dotted amongst the trees. Grovelands was to be the clubhouse set in a private parkland. However, the scheme ran out of steam and never materialised.

As it was, the delays had given the Southgate Urban District

Council the necessary time to gather their thoughts and ideas about the future of this most beautiful part of their region. They decided to go ahead with their own plans to create another park. At least a fraction of Taylor's legacy would be safeguarded for the future. They purchased 64 acres in 1911 for £22,893, and have since increased this to 91 acres. As with Broomfield 10 years earlier, there was vociferous opposition to the scheme, with fears of heavy rate rises. The bulk of Lot 9 was eventually made up and developed, but we still have Grovelands Park as our heritage.

What a debt past, present and future generations owe to those wise councillors, who had the foresight to preserve some open spaces, when all around bricks and mortar were spreading over a once green countryside.

Grovelands Park was officially opened on 12th April 1913, by the Lord Mayor, Sir David Burnett.

Following the outbreak of the First World War, Captain Taylor, with encouragement from his wife, agreed to let the house and immediate grounds rent free to the Southgate branch of the Middlesex Voluntary Aid Organisation, for use as an auxiliary hospital for wounded soldiers for 'as long as it should be required'. In a short time, they had equipped the house to take up to 70 patients, and it opened as a hospital on 17th June 1916.

Captain Taylor's generosity, and the great efforts of the Southgate VAO, combined to make the venture a great success and many a wounded soldier had treatment, and was restored to good health, in these most pleasant surroundings.

After the war, Captain Taylor decided to sell and, in 1921, the Southgate VAO purchased the house and gardens with funds they had raised during war-time. They handed it over to the Great (later the Royal) Northern Group of Voluntary Hospitals, for use in patients' treatment and convalescence. The agreement was that, if ever the building should cease to be used as a hospital, it should pass to Southgate Council.

Relying on the hard work and fund raising efforts of many local people, the hospital continued its good work through World War II. After hostilities, Grovelands was taken over by the State, when the National Health Service was established and then, under re-organisation in 1974, the new Enfield & Haringey Area Health Authority took responsibility.

It wasn't long before its future was in doubt, with economies having to be made and, early in 1977, the axe fell. After 61 years service, the hospital closed.

A very sorry chapter began after the closure of the hospital. Grovelands Park was still there to enjoy, a beautiful sight still but, behind the fence and the ha-ha that once served to keep the herds of wild deer from straying too near this once great mansion, the signs of decay and neglect were only too apparent. The empty house was deteriorating before our eyes and prospective buyers were shy, no doubt, of the mounting sums that would be needed to put the place in good order. There were obvious limitations as to the practical use of such a building, and the future looked far from bright.

Then, in 1985, came the good news. We heard that Community Psychiatric Centres (C.P.C.)*, a British subsidiary of an American company, was interested in acquiring the building and 8 acres of ground, to run as Grovelands Priory Hospital, providing 65 beds for patients suffering short term mental illnesses. The security men moved out and, after some delay, the builders moved in. Following 8 barren years, work was underway.

Annexes were built at the rear to house the patients' bedrooms. The house itself, which is used mainly for administrative services and consulting rooms, has been restored to its former glory. On a recent visit it did my heart good to see the house alive again and serving such a useful purpose.

One lovely autumn afternoon in 1986, just before the official opening on Sunday 19th October, I stood in the lounge, looking out of the windows through the colonnade and across the lake to the woods beyond. It was a scene of great beauty and tranquillity. I remembered the rowing boats we would hire from the boathouse on a summer's afternoon, when I was a lad, and our trips around the lake. Regrettably, in recent years, vandalism has put paid to such pleasures.

I explored the famous birdcage room, originally the breakfast room. It was designed with a vaulted ceiling, and had been beautifully decorated to resemble a birdcage with creepers entwined around the bars. It had been painstakingly restored, and I am sure 'JDT' would have approved.

Elsewhere, in the entrance hallway and up the grand staircase, the builders were busy applying the final touches ready for the deadline a few days hence. I came away so pleased to think that a building, that had been dying, had been revived and would go on living for many years to come.

*The name has since been changed to Priory Hospitals Group and the present Director is Mr. Richard Foulkes.

A few months later, in January 1987, Tony Lewis of C.P.C. kindly invited me to go over the house, now fulfilling its role and caring for its patients. I was most impressed, both by the way the original house has been so faithfully restored, and by the new buildings, which have been so carefully designed to blend in with the original. I was able to see the old plans of the house, which indicated the function of each room back in Taylor's time and before. The old adjustable book shelves are still there, in what once had been a Library, and is now part of the Dining Room. Throughout, the reinstatement of the ornamental cornices has been meticulous.

As well as money, a great deal of care and thought has gone into the project. There was work to the grounds still scheduled to be done, but the will is there to carry it through.

I was most intrigued by my visit to the basement, where one can see an intricate pattern of brick vaulted foundations, with an old ice chamber recalling bygone days before electricity and refrigeration, and an underground drainage ditch or moat girthing the old house. There was evidence, too, of the recent extensive work carried out to combat the ravages of dry rot. It was a most welcome and reassuring visit to one of Southgate's great historic houses.

In fact, I have written sparingly about the house or indeed the park itself – whilst they are still there and capable of being seen, it seems unnecessary to describe their features. As part of our heritage, may they both remain for many years to come.

Beyond the ha-ha is the vista of Grovelands Park. A picturesque spot from whichever view you take, what else has it to offer? A little corner of Winchmore Hill Woods that still survives; walks in the fresh air through undulating fields; the quaint old Tea House; a small 9 hole course to test our pitching and putting skills; and the centrepiece, Grovelands Lake, a fine stretch of water girthed by trees and shady paths where young fishermen still while away some happy hours. Treasured moments indeed.

It would be fun, wouldn't it, to go back in time to the great days of the Walkers and the Taylors and view the scene. Those great cricket matches on Chapel Fields (now the Walker Ground) when Southgate was a mecca for the sport. When all the great cricketers in England would gather in this quiet village to the north of London to play against the men of Southgate. Crowds of 10,000 would flock to witness these great social and sporting occasions, which were so much more than mere cricket matches spread over 3 days in August. There was always a great carnival atmosphere with flags and bunting in profusion. There would be other sporting contests going on, a brass military band in full regalia, and everyone dressed in their Sunday best.

The hosts and organisers of these great events were the Walker brothers. All seven were highly talented at the sport – fine men who gave so much to cricket and to Southgate. The generosity of their hospitality became renowned. Their lovely home, Arnos Grove, would be thrown open for their guests to use. Looking south across their estate and the Pymmes Brook valley, scarcely a house could be seen. It was a picture of great beauty and charm. London, it seemed, was a thousand miles away.

The Walkers and the Taylors had a great affinity. They were related by marriage and united in business in the brewery that today still bears their names. But most important of all was their alliance in policy as landowners.

They both bought up land as it became available to gradually, step by step, increase the size of their estates. By these methods they retained control. Their road frontages were not built upon, the developers were scorned and the railway and public transport authorities were held at bay. Both parties did their utmost to retain the rural scene in our area and, to a considerable degree, they were successful.

Some would question their motives. Some would suggest it was self-interest, but it is easy to brand any conservationist in this way. The Walkers and the Taylors were highly respected and admired by the local people, and they contributed a great deal to community life in many different ways. They loved the area as it was and would do all they could to preserve it. They had become the guardians of the future and their battle was fought for the benefit of all.

On that fateful day in June 1902, when the Taylor estates went up for sale, there were just two of the Walker brothers still alive. Vyell Edward, head of the Arnos Grove household, was 65, his brother Russell just 60.

One wonders on their thoughts that day. All seven brothers had remained bachelors and five of them had passed on, leaving no heirs. The watershed had been reached. The developers were moving in and there could be no turning back. They were powerless to stop it. After 125 years the Walker presence in Southgate was drawing to a close. It must have been a sad realisation after their invaluable contribution to village life.

V.E. Walker did attend the sale and entered the bidding for Lot No.13 (The Waterfall Estate) to no avail. It would have been easy for them to have been resentful at this time, but there is no such indication. V.E. (Edward) Walker, in particular, continued to do all he could to make the transition period as painless as possible. His every action seemed to have the villagers' interests at heart. And so the line petered out, but The Walkers of Southgate will forever be spoken of with pride and affection.

The other half of the partnership, the Taylors, had an even more direct bearing on the Winchmore Hill area. I have written elsewhere of the delightful walk to All Saints Church that the Southgate villagers would make, before the Weld Chapel was built in 1615. The walk remained a great favourite even into the twentieth century, for it led us to the village of Winchmore Hill and beyond into Edmonton.

We would go down the footpath (now known as The Mall) alongside the Cherry Tree Inn and across some open fields, through a clap gate, where Oakfield Road now joins, and into the woods. Before the hamlet of Clappers Green, we would take the left fork at a divided footpath, which led us into Fox Lane by the Village Pound. Across Dog & Duck Lane, we would go through another stile and on to another footpath (now Broad Walk). We are walking now in dense woodland, deep in the heart of Mr. Taylor's territory.

There is a picket fence on our left, marking the boundary of the Grovelands Estate and, further west, the more open aspect of a beautiful lake and the mansion itself. We may be lucky to sight some of the wild deer that once roamed these parts. The 1897 O.S. Map still marks the area as Deer Park. To the east, on the north side of Dog & Duck Lane, the woods extend as far as Hoppers Road.

We have come some 300 yards since crossing the stile and there, on the left, would be the gamekeeper's cottage, known locally as Keeper's Cottage and marked on some of the old maps as Wood Cottage. The early photographers have recorded the scene for it was such a delightful spot. Its position was opposite the Brackendale of today, where White Timbers now stands. We are still in dense forest, Miss Cresswell's magical playground of over a hundred years ago.

In my research I discovered that, for centuries, this area provided work for many of the villagers. As early as the thirteenth century, there were areas designated as coppice wood. The trees were allowed to grow and would be cut in rotation every ten years. Much of it was then sold as logwood in 4 feet lengths, as fuel for the broad hearths. The shreddings were bound into faggots, many of them being sold to bakers for use in heating their large ovens. The bark was peeled and sold to the tanneries in Enfield and Edmonton.

The Keeper's Cottage, which stood by the side of the footpath, opposite to today's Brackendale.

Broad Walk in the mid 1930's had still not been made up.

The Winchmore Hill end of the footpath, looking towards Wood Corner.

Some of the wood was used for making charcoal by the 'colyers' (charcoal burners) of Winchmore Hill. This was a very old and highly skilled occupation, usually handed down within the family and through the generations.

Clamps would be made by propping up logs of even length against a central post, which was later withdrawn. The whole clamp, shaped like an igloo, would be covered with mould and leaves and then fired with a burning torch inserted into its heart. It was essential that a slow, carefully controlled, combustion took place, usually spread over 7 to 10 days and nights. The burners would camp out in the woods next to their clamps, on constant watch. They would carefully control the rate of burning using turf, leaves and sacking as their 'dampers', for too quick or too slow a burn would impair the quality of the final product. Once the cooling process had been completed, the charcoal would be extracted and bagged up, ready for sale.

Charcoal was at one time a valuable fuel, used extensively in our blast furnaces for iron smelting, but its importance declined with the introduction of coke. Gas and oil are other fuels that have come to replace charcoal as the years have gone by. Its use today is restricted to small and specialist application, such as case hardening, fireworks, barbecue fuel, insulating material, filtering agent, and in medicines. Though the trade has largely died, it is as well that we remember the charcoal burners of Winchmore Hill, for they once played an important part in the life of our village.

There is little to remind us today of the great forest that once covered these parts but some corners of it do remain. The best approach is to enter the park via the Seaforth Gardens entrance. We are immediately surrounded by woods, stretching across to the lake and down to the stream, which still gurgles on its way. We can look across the lake towards the big house and still appreciate its beauty. As we stroll around the lake, away from the traffic, the air has a slightly fresher tang, no doubt appreciated by the wild life that makes its haven here.

And so the destiny of Lot Number 9 was gradually settled. With the opening of the park in 1913 and the conversion of the mansion into a hospital in 1916, it only remained for the development of Broad Walk and the roads to the east to settle its fate.

Once upon a time there was a footpath through the woods that had been walked since time immemorial. That footpath became Broad Walk. In 1912, Wood Corner, a small gathering of cottages fronted by Mummery's shop looking out onto the Green, was demolished. This was to make way for the new avenue that was to run between the Green and Bourne Hill, on the line of the old footpath. Even after the roadway was completed, the development of this last fragment of Taylor's holdings went ahead slowly, stage by stage, well into the 1930's.

This was in marked contrast, for instance, to the Old Park estate in Palmers Green (Lot No.1, bought by the British Land Company in 1902). Here, roads and housing were spreading at an amazing rate. Similarly, the sale of Clappers Green Farm in 1908 had prompted immediate response from the builders. Consequently, this corner of Palmers Green between Aldermans Hill and Dog & Duck Lane (Bourne Hill) had been fully exploited and developed by 1911/12, well before the outbreak of war.

This must have been the heyday for our local architects, planners, developers and builders. There was so much work to be done and they responded, let it be said, with great energy and purpose.

Gradually, Woodland Way and the network of roads linking up with Broad Walk took shape. The houses were well designed and a credit to the builder. Some had pleasant open aspects at the rear, backing on to the two sports grounds included in the plans.

The development of Broad Walk was a very slow process. True, the line and width of the new unsurfaced road had been established well before 1914, but building work on the prestigous plots went ahead slowly through the late twenties, and into the thirties. One of our local residents, Miss Tewson, who taught my wife at St. Olave's School many years ago, was kind enough to show me photographs, revealing how the road looked as the big houses gradually took shape, filling some of the building plots. Miss Tewson's parents were the first occupiers of number 62 Broad Walk in 1932, when the purchase price was £3,500. As the pictures reveal, Miss Tewson, then a teenager, clearly recalls the roadway as being full of potholes and puddles.

Thereby hangs a tale, for the local authority, at the time, was denying responsibility for making up the road. In 1936, Southgate Borough Council was engaged in a law suit with the residents of Broad Walk. The Council had served notice on the owners requiring them to make up the road. The owners, in turn, sought a declaration from the High Court that the cost of making it up should be borne by the ratepayers of Southgate at large. Learned Counsel were employed on both sides. The case took two days to hear, on conclusion of which the judge, Mr. Justice Porter (who became Lord Porter) reserved his judgement. Some months later, judgement was made in favour of the Council. Afterwards the two parties agreed to compromise and, in 1936/7, the road was at last properly made up and lit.

The detached Broad Walk residences were something special, and remain so, each one with its own style and character. It was generally recognised as the 'posh' road in the district, which the locals were quick to dub 'Millionaires' Row'. With mature trees lining the verges, its unique herringbone, redbricked pavements and most attractive lampposts, it was a pleasure to stroll along in the cool of a summer's evening before entering the park. I can well remember such walks with my parents, when we would pretend we had won the football pools and could choose the house of our dreams. Such fantasies continued as I grew up. It was a game many of us played then and, I suppose, still do.

What of Broad Walk today? It has, I suspect, lost some of its pre-war grandeur. The hurricane of October 1987 took its toll. Several of the mature trees were affected. Some were lost and others disfigured with limbs torn off like so much matchwood. The pavements no longer have that pristine look and even the quaint old lampposts have been replaced. The empty plots have now been filled and the traffic hurries by on, what is now, a busy road.

It is still a lovely setting, however, with some fine houses and colourful gardens to delight the eye. The woods and the old footpath may have gone forever but, let us enter Grovelands one summer's morn when the mist is still above the lake. All is still and we are at peace with nature. Was that a glimpse of Mr. Taylor walking in the grounds, or could it be a trick of the early light? Our echoed call rings out unanswered. Has he come to take his last look round at all he loved so dearly? His image fades into the mist and is lost from our sight.

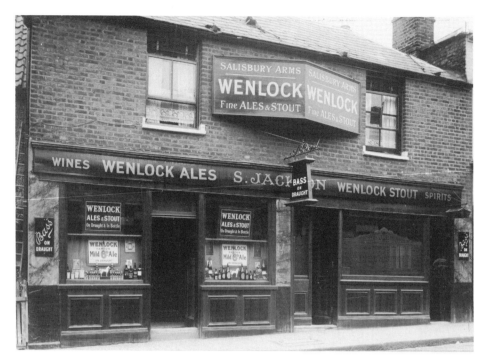

The old Salisbury Arms.

The new Salisbury Arms opened for business in February 1936.

# CHAPTER 3

## THE VILLAGE CENTRE

WINCHMORE HILL GREEN was originally of far greater size and of far greater importance than it is today. The widening of the many roads that surround it, and the creation of pavements and other encroachments has gradually whittled the area away to less than half its original size. The volume of traffic, which today negotiates the area, could never have been envisaged in times gone by, and the parking and congestion problems continue to increase, as they do throughout all our built-up areas.

However, the Green remains the focal point where 5 major roads (Hoppers Road, Broad Walk, Church Hill, Wades Hill and Station Road) now converge, with subsidiary roads, such as Compton Road and Vicars Moor Lane, feeding into these thoroughfares a short distance away.

At the turn of the century, we still had the village pond, situated on the eastern section of the Green. Once it was very picturesque, with ducks and geese swimming contentedly on its waters. It was surrounded by pollarded willow trees, with an opening on the south side, where horses and carts could pull in to cool down in the heat of a summer's day, and have a free wash simultaneously.

In the early 1800's, adjacent to the pond, stood a conventional windlass-operated well which, together with the vicar's well in Vicars Moor Lane, provided fresh water for the village. In 1850, a terrible tragedy occurred on the Green, when a little child fell into the well and was drowned. This prompted Mrs. Todd, who lived at Uplands, the very large residence facing on to the Green, to donate the money required for the well to be phased out, and be replaced by a hand pump.

Eventually, around 1883, a piped water supply began to be laid in the village and gradually the pump became neglected and disused. It was replaced by a standpipe, which gave many years of good service and was used for washing the roads down, and filling up the water carts, horsetroughs etc. A few years later, the gas supplies began to be laid and lampposts were erected on some of the main roads, including the Green, to provide much needed illumination.

The pond became rather polluted and, in 1908, the Council filled it in and replaced it with a much smaller, artificially enclosed pond, situated nearer to Hoppers Road, complete with a fountain. There are many postcards of this period showing the Green and its fountain, with the posts and protective rails around the grassed areas. These had all been erected some years earlier.

The Green was used much more for community activities in the old days. Since the time of King Edward III, who was crowned in 1327, it is said that a fair was regularly held on the Green, near the Kings Head. Centuries later, this was moved but, early in the 1700's, another fair began and was extended to 3 days with a variety of sideshows to amuse the villagers. The area in front of the Limes and Uplands (i.e. the western portion) would be used by the boys for cricket matches and, even after the fair had ceased to operate, a variety of itinerant traders would regularly visit the village and ply their wares on the Green to an attentive audience.

Miss Cresswell tells us of the 'Cart on the Green', where the wonders of photography were introduced to her in the 1860's and Regnart recalls the regular visits of an American called Sequah, in the 1880's. What a thrill that must have been for the locals, most of whom had travelled little beyond their own surroundings. Sequah sold bottles of a magical liniment that was a cure for all ailments. As a sideline, he pulled out teeth free of charge. He always brought with him a brass band, which started to play once you had mounted a waggon and were seated ready for tooth extraction. It is not recorded whether the band was there to pacify the patients, or merely to drown their screams!

The Green became an ideal meeting place for politicians, where they could canvass for votes and air their views to a somewhat critical audience, who were liable to barrack the speaker when they felt it was warranted. Electioneering brought forth argument and counter-argument, much as it does today. There would be other open-air meetings on religious and temperance themes, similar to those we still associate with Speakers' Corner in Hyde Park.

Those who spoke on the evils of drink did so at their peril. The Taylors, the Walkers, the Manns and the Paulins, whose family wealth was based on the brewery trade, were highly respected local gentry. Their generosity had aided the community for decades, in many different ways. To criticise them, or their motives, inevitably led to a very heated debate.

Village festivals and celebrations would be centred on the Green, including a huge bonfire on Guy Fawkes night. When the pond froze in the winter time, there would be skating on the ice and some impromptu slides for the youngsters. Traditionally, the heart of an English village lay at the Green, where the locals danced around the Maypole and chose their queen of the May. Winchmore Hill was no exception.

It will become apparent that I have covered much of Hoppers Road in later chapters, excepting the northern end, near the junction with Compton Road. I shall explore that area in this chapter, for it can truthfully be termed part of the village centre. This will start us on our journey that will continue, in the broadest of terms, with a clockwise rotation of the Green. These are mere guidelines. I have tried to avoid repetition of ground I have already covered, and hope I have maintained a logical sequence, in spite of great difficulties.

For instance, the seeds of the Congregational Church were sown at Wood Corner, which were then transplanted to two sites in Hoppers Road, coming to fruition eventually in Compton Road. One has to write its history in continuity, which necessitates quite rapid change of direction. I hope you follow my thoughts.

There will inevitably be some omissions of people, places and events. To cover an area so rich in history in greater detail, would require a volume much weightier than mine. Hopefully, I have included the main points of interest, relevant to the development of our village. Let us make a start in Hoppers Road.

The Salisbury Arms, like the Green Dragon Hotel, has moved around during its lifetime under different guises. The public house was originally situated nearer the Green than it is today, i.e. where Salisbury Court and the adjoining garages are now situated.

Why was the inn so named? Some historians point to the aged and somewhat eccentric dowager Marchioness of Salisbury who lived at Hatfield House. There, in 1835, she accidentally started a fire and burnt herself and most of the West Wing of the mansion. Lord Salisbury tried again and again to fight his way through to his mother's room, only to be beaten back by the flames. Also, it is suggested, one of the estate workers made an heroic, but unsuccessful, attempt to save her, and for this he was rewarded by being set up in a small inn at Winchmore Hill, which he named the Salisbury Arms. The connection cannot be proven.

In 1852, a new butchers shop, Alfred Stockton, was built on the site of what is thought to have been the original ale house, the basement cellars of which were retained. The premises next door on the south side, originally a butchers shop, were then converted into a public house.

We have photographs of this, the second Salisbury Arms, showing a plain two-storey building, about the width of two shops, clearly functioning as a combined off-licence and public house. The fascia reads 'Wenlock Ales, S. Jackson', and one shop window displays bottled beers, whereas the other is covered with an acid-embossed screen reading 'Wines & Spirits'. A pair of doors gives access to the bar. Wenlock's Mild Ale on draught is advertised in the window at 6d (2½p) per pint and draught Bass was also available. Alfred Stockton, the butchers, adjoins the pub on its northern side, nearer to The Green. On the opposite side of the road was a tall signpost, advertising the presence of the inn.

It was in 1935 that Wenlock's Brewery built the fine new building, that we know today as the Salisbury Arms. Years ago, this site was occupied by Belmont House, a tall imposing dwelling, set well back from the road, with iron railings set in the dwarf wall protecting the front garden. Mature trees and high shrubs sheltered the house, which was a private residence for most of its life, but was used, for a time, as a girls' school. Adjoining Belmont House, to the north, were some modest dwellings known as Taylors and Salisbury Cottages. They were slightly forward of Belmont House, yet still with room enough for flowering shrubs to fill their front gardens lining Hoppers Road. In front of them all was the triangle of green, with the lovely horse chestnut tree that survives to this day.

This more modest Salisbury Arms, that I have described, served its last pint on Friday night, 14th February 1936. Its fine new successor opened for trade the very next day and has continued to serve us with distinction to the present time. Belmont House and the cottages are but a memory.

Holly Lodge, too, is but a memory, but of more recent times. This small 18th century house, of unusual design for its years, was set in a fine landscaped garden on the southern corner of Compton Road and Hoppers Road. A familiar tar-coated fence lined its boundary with Hoppers Road, and led to a small wooden barn. At one time, the house was the home of Mr. Claringbull, the engineer in charge of the building of the railway, the arrival of which, in 1871, must have disturbed the tranquillity of this once quiet retreat. Holly Lodge was demolished in 1972 to make way for a block of flats.

Compton Road (once called Front Lane) was named after a lawyer, Samuel Compton, who lived in a house about half-way down on the south side. When he died in 1840, the house was pulled down and the ground added to Highfield Park, more details of which will be found in Chapter 6. Very little development took place in Compton Road until after the turn of the century.

The site of Compton Terrace was once an open field. A wooden barn with a red-tiled roof featured at the Compton Road end and, adjacent to the bakery, was a yard where the old Salisbury Arms signpost stood, advertising the presence of the inn opposite. To the

Looking towards the Green from Hoppers Road, showing Compton Terrace.

31

Hoppers Road looking south, showing the familiar triangle and the horse chestnut tree c1920.

Chalkley's Farmhouse Bakery & their shop on the corner.

north of the bakehouse, where the shops now exist, round to the Roseville entrance, was formerly a very colourful front garden belonging to the Village Bakery which dates back to c1720.

At one time, the two Miss Catchpoles* owned the bakery. As a sideline they were successful beekeepers and produced fine quality honey. Miss Cresswell tells an amusing story that one year, with an abundance of honey being available, they turned their hand to making mead. Sister Lydia decided she should sample the new product. The nectar tasted so sweet and so innocuous that, before she realised it, she had over-indulged. She awoke next morning, sitting in front of a now empty grate and described the newly discovered mead as 'powerfully refreshing'.

The Catchpoles were Quakers, as were their successors Mr. and Mrs. Burns, who eventually left the bakery to run a dairy farm further down Hoppers Road. The Goldsworthy family ran the business for some time and, last of all, came the Chalkleys. The Chalkleys already had a bakers shop in Middle Lane (Station Road), where they had succeeded Mr. Stern round about 1880. Now, on the death of Mr. Goldsworthy, they bought the business and moved in to Hoppers Road. Their old shop in Middle Lane became Press, the newsagents.

Many of my readers will have recollections of the Chalkleys, a highly respected family, and their shop on the corner, for the business continued to operate right through the wartime years, with an ever-cheerful Mrs. Chalkley coping with our demands for bread and cakes.

I understand the bakehouse ovens ceased to operate from about 1945, though the corner baker's shop continued to trade into the 1960's, since when it has changed hands many times. The old bakery itself has seen changes, too. It was converted into an antique shop in post war years, when a doorway and shop enclosure was formed in Hoppers Road. The original entrance is reached by going down a narrow passage on the north side.

It was here that Mrs. Anstee, the present owner, greeted me and kindly took me over the premises which are now purely residential. It was a most interesting visit for, though the old bakery had undergone many fundamental changes, it is still possible to see parts of the original and, with imagination, to picture the rest as it existed centuries ago.

The main beam and joists are made of oak, said to be so hard that

*On the bakery's legal documents apertaining to the lease etc., the name is sometimes spelt Catchpool.

a nail will not penetrate. There is still evidence of the old original oven with its curved and domed walls, where once the villagers' bread was baked, and the more recent oven where the inscription J.C. 1822 is clearly marked. The loading bay door on the south side still prevails, though no longer are the sacks of flour hauled up by rope and pulley, to be guided in and loaded on to racks. Down in the basement, we removed the cover to expose the well. I was told the water had been analysed as pure. Its level, which scarcely varies whatever the season, is only a few inches below the basement floor.

We went out by the back door into the alley that runs alongside and behind the cottages, to see the old stables and straw-house, where once the baker's steeds could rest content. I took my leave, so grateful to Mrs. Anstee for allowing me this glimpse into our past.

The other corner of Hoppers Road was always known, in my youth, as Tidey's or Dicky Bird corner. Then, Dicky Bird was the corner sweet shop, though it had previously been Tidey's which, in turn, became the newspaper shop just round the corner in Hoppers Road. It was quite an experience to enter either shop. One was entering a time capsule, and going back to the turn of the century. Tidey's shop projected in front of the building line in Hoppers Road, leaving a very narrow pavement to negotiate.

Above Dicky Bird, going towards Broad Walk, there were two more shops and then, originally, some old clapboarded cottages, set well back, with long front gardens, before we came to the draper's shop, now the dental surgery. The old cottages were subsequently demolished to make way for Cookley House, built in 1927 to accommodate the builders, H.J. Maynard & Sons. These premises, officially No. 29, are now used as commercial offices.

The demolition of the corner in 1965 was a grievous blow. The old buildings had great character and appeal, and the void created was like a wound that would never heal. A vital part of the old village had gone for ever.

Compton Terrace, a row of artisan houses of great charm and appeal, remain. These occupy the site between the bakery and the railway bridge and were built by Mr. Butson around 1883.

Within my memory, the dwelling nearest to Compton Road, which is called Hillsboro (No. 13) has always been a ladies hairdressers. Many readers will remember this as Maison Ivy and others will recall 'Dorothy' (Mrs. Adams), who continued the business from 1963 until 1986, when it reverted to a private residence.

John James Butson was a builder, who lived at one time in Winchmore Hill Road (then called Chase Side). In 1883, he came to live at Woodside, a large house near Wood Corner, alongside a footpath that led through Winchmore Hill Woods. We know the house today as Nos. 35 & 37 The Green or, by name, as Rowantree House and Woodside House. The earliest deed relating to the property is dated 1786, but the document records 6 previous owners or tenants, so the house could easily be 250 years old.

Originally, Rowantree and Woodside were one house called Woodside. The property included a pair of old cottages next door where, it is said, a forge had previously operated from c1650. This is difficult to prove. The premises were extended for use as a shop from about 1840 and, following several alterations over the years to suit a variety of purposes, they currently operate as a Dental Surgery. There had been a large orchard and a field at the back, where a block of flats has subsequently been built.

There was a long period when Woodside was let out to a succession of tenants. One of these, Mr. Neville, adopted his mother's maiden name for anonymity. He was the son of Mr. Bellingham, the man who assassinated our Prime Minister, Spencer Perceval, in the lobby of the House of Commons in 1812. Mr. Neville tried to escape from the disgrace he felt by living in a quiet country village, but it was to no avail. He became a reclusive, lonely figure and his remorse turned to depression and despair. The tragedy was compounded by his ultimate suicide at Woodside.

After Mr. Butson had purchased the estate in 1883 for £2,000, he set about dividing the house into two. One part he named Rowantree (No. 35) and the other retained the original name of Woodside (No. 37). The shop and cottage becoming vacant, he let it out to Mr. G. Richards, a draper of Shepherds Bush, for £40 per annum, on a lease of 21 years.

John Butson lived at Rowantree until 1894, when he let it to Dr. Jackson, who came from Oakbank, a house next to Roseville, since converted into a shop. Dr. Jackson practised in Winchmore Hill for 23 years but, owing to ill health, he gave up his local practise to become a ship's doctor. He died at Mombasa in 1914, and there is a memorial to him in St. Paul's Church, erected by his wife and children.

The property was sold to George Lacey of Palmers Green. He sold Woodside to Mrs. Tyson in 1903 and retained the rest of the property, including Rowantree, which remained in his family until 1947.

There is something appealing about an old-fashioned drapers

shop and Mably's as it became after Richards', was no exception. Many of my readers will doubtless recall it with pleasure, even possibly from the depths of their dentist's chair. We are indeed fortunate to have such historic buildings still surviving.

On the other hand, the old properties at Wood Corner, on the north side of the footpath, have not survived. The shop known as Mummery's, a cabinet and house furnishing concern, run by Mr. A.H. Mummery, was demolished in 1911/12 to make way for a new thoroughfare, later to be known as Broad Walk. They originally dealt in many spheres, as house agents, removers, storers, shippers, upholsterers, funeral directors etc. before these trades became more specialised. The business moved to 63 Station Road, just downhill from the station on the opposite side of the road, where it traded for many years as a house furnishers of high repute and good quality. The shop is currently a Fish Bar and Kebab House.

It would be of interest, I feel, to establish the position of the old Mummery's shop at Wood Corner. The shop front, which faced onto the Green, was on the line of the garage attached on the western side of Woodside. That line can be further identified by a tall conifer, which currently grows alongside this garage. The footpath thus ran to the south of the flank wall of the shop, which occupied the remaining width of what is Broad Walk today.

Before Mummery's the shop had been Udall & Childs, a shop of great renown, where contraband goods such as foreign silks and laces, brandy, tea and tobacco were sold. Obviously, these were goods normally liable to very high duty. They were smuggled in on pack horses, across the Essex and Hackney Marshes, to this remote hamlet of Winchmore Hill, well beyond the reach of the customs and excise inspectors of the day. Some of our old villagers mention tales of mysterious underground tunnels in this area. Were they lines of supply for the contraband, or merely secret hiding places? Has the legend any substance, or are the tunnels a myth?

Charles and Mary Lamb were regular customers, and friends of the Udalls, and they would walk to Winchmore Hill Green from their home in Gentlemans Row and Chase Side, Enfield, across the fields and orchards of Pike's Farm. Udall's reputation for matchless linens and fabrics, as well as rare old china, spread beyond the village. The fine carriages of the well-to-do and the famous could sometimes be spotted on the Green, whilst their owners chose from the many treasures on offer in the shop.

Mrs. Childs was the last of the Udalls to run the shop, before it became Mummery's. It was a quaint old-fashioned shop, built tight

Winchmore Hill Green 1884. We can just pick out the village pump (centre) and Roseville (extreme right).

Mably's old shop has become a Dental Surgery, whilst Rowantree House and
Woodside House still survive.

The old Mummery's shop at Wood Corner, where once had been Udalls & Childs.
A very historic part of the old village.

to the footpath. The shop window was divided into 21 panes of glass. In the distance, on its left, was the wooden gate where one entered the woods. Attached to the right of the shop and set back, were the living quarters and outbuildings. A portico and extended porchway led to the entrance. The premises had an extensive cellar and a most interesting safe which was housed within the brick enclosure of a basement well. To gain access, the safe had to be raised by means of chain and tackle, later to be returned to its 'secret' hiding place.

The Udall family were prominent tradesmen in the village, in many different spheres. Around 1830, they formed their own religious sect, called the Udallites, and established their own tiny chapel in Vicars Moor Lane. I do not know of their special beliefs or religious attitudes, but the sect did not endure and the chapel was taken over by the strict Baptists in the 1860's and was rebuilt in 1883. In recent years, the number of worshippers dwindled and closure became inevitable. The last service was held on Sunday, 29th August 1982 with four in attendance. The chapel has since been converted for private residential use though, being a listed building, the external fabric remains.

Behind Mummery's, the little cul-de-sac leading up to Wood Gate was lined with small dwellings, and the area was known as Wood Corner.

A feature of a developing village, at this time, was the movement of some of the family enterprises. Aldridge's, the greengrocers, started in a tiny shop next to Mummery's. The business later transferred to a shop near Tidey's corner, next to the old cottages, facing the Green. Then, within living memory, the next generation moved on to Wades Hill and a shop in Station Road, nearly opposite the station. I can remember the latter and Mr. Aldridge, a most affable proprietor, always happy to pass the time of day with his regular customers.

Aldridge's shop at Wood Corner became John Downes', the corn merchants, who later moved to a shop on the Green (No. 16, now Elizabeth's, the florists). The name of Downes Court reminds us of the family's close local connections over a long period. John Downes was born in a cottage at the southern end of Hoppers Road. His father had been a gardener for the Walkers at Arnos Grove for over 40 years and his son James, who lived at Busks Cottages and latterly in Highfield Road, was a stoker at Highlands Hospital. In 1949, James and his wife Mary celebrated their Diamond Wedding.

Adjacent to Downes' shop at Wood Corner, were the Woodside

Cottages, built on the site of the old Independent Meeting House. Beyond, lay Winchmore Hill Woods and the footpath to Dog & Duck Lane.

Aldridge's greengrocers shop near Tidey's corner became Riley's the grocers, which also served as the village Post Office. This enterprise moved across the Green, opposite the Kings Head, in about 1880. The other shops at the top of Wades Hill were built a few years later.

In reading about village life and its tradespeople, the same names crop up, time and time again. The Aldridges and the Downes are typical examples. It tells us that generation followed generation, born into an environment where they, and their children, would probably remain. The villagers were unlikely, or unable, to journey far afield. The ease of travel we take for granted today, was yet to come.

The facts relating to the origins of the Independent Church in Winchmore Hill are a little uncertain. There is no doubt, however, that the establishment of an Independent Chapel at Wood Corner, as a house of worship, was second only to the Friends Meeting House in Church Hill (1688).

I have explained that Wood Corner lay on the western side of the Green, where Broad Walk now joins. As we know, in years gone by, Broad Walk was merely a footpath through Winchmore Hill Woods and a narrow opening, by the side of Udalls shop, led out to the open Green beyond. Adjacent, and behind the shop, were a few wooden dwellings which included the Old Independent Meeting House, which appears to have been founded in 1742.

This date has been arrived at after a great deal of detailed research. There is no doubt that the Meeting House was operating in the latter half of the 18th century, and that the lease was due to expire at Midsummer 1841. It was common practice for leases to have a 99 years duration at this time and so, by deduction, 1742 appears to be the likely date of foundation. In fact, an extension to the lease was granted and worship continued there until September 1843. Thereafter, for a period of about 11 months, worship continued 'on the premises of a friend to the Redeemer's Cause in the hope that a new sanctuary would be built.'

Fortunately there is a sketch of the old chapel in existence, which shows a small, wooden building with a low-pitched, gabled roof and two windows, with their shutters folded back. The building line is set back from the cottage next door (thought to be the home of John Radford, Deacon of the Church), forming a small enclosure, fronted by a dwarf wall. The end wall, against which a tiny lean-to rests, features two segmental-arched windows and a modest bell-tower, projecting above the rear slope. These features alone identify it as a house of worship, rather than a private dwelling.

In the early 1840's, there was work to be done, for the Independents had to find a new home. A fund was opened. Letters of appeal, signed by the Pastor, H. Pawling and the Deacon, John Radford, were distributed and the building of a new sanctuary in Hoppers Road began. This opened for public worship on Tuesday, 13th August 1844, when John Harris, President of Cheshunt College, preached the opening sermon at 11 a.m. and George Clayton, of Walworth, conducted the evening service at 6 p.m. At the time, only one quarter of the building costs had been raised and a further appeal was made for assistance 'to all who love our Lord Jesus, so that not only the present generation, but also future generations shall rise up to call the Redeemer Blessed'.

There is evidence that the old Independent Meeting House was demolished by John Radford in 1848, i.e. 4 years after the move to Hoppers Road, which infers that he was the owner or trustee of the building and that his ancestors may have granted the original lease.

The demolition of the chapel and the preparation for some cottages to be erected on the site, revealed evidence of an old burial ground. You may recall that a similar discovery was made in 1937, when the chapel in Chase Side, Southgate (originally owned by the Independents) was demolished, leading to a delay in building operations. At Wood Corner, some of the old timbers were salvaged and re-used in the construction of the cottages. The stairs in one, it was said, once served the Minister in his climb to the pulpit.

The new sanctuary, officially the New Independent Chapel of Winchmore Hill, was situated on the eastern side of Hoppers Road, where the skew bridge now spans the railway, nearly opposite Downes Court. It was next door and just to the north of Trois Vase house, the home of Doctor Cresswell. The chapel was a white brick building of more ambitious ecclesiastical design than its predecessor, with high Gothic pinnacles and long lancet windows. It was set well back from the road, in very rural surroundings, with laurel bushes marking the boundary of the property. In 1846, the Rev. J. Charles Richards was appointed Minister. The new chapel was to last but a quarter of a century for, on 1st January 1870, the Church authorities had to vacate the premises prior to demolition. This was to make way for the coming of the railway, described in more detail in Chapter 5.

At this time a temporary 'Iron Chapel', constructed of corrugated iron, was erected on ground allocated to the authorities by the Great Northern Railway, for a rent free period of 2 years, as from 21st October 1869. I have very little information about this building, except that it was 20 feet wide and 32 feet deep, with a central entrance porchway. However, I have been able to establish its position. It was built on a triangular plot of land on the western side of Hoppers Road, just to the south of the skew bridge, tight up to the railway cutting. The chapel was roughly opposite 186/188 Hoppers Road, where some lock-up garages now exist.

The events leading up to the transfer and creation of the new church at the top of Compton Road, as we know it today, are open to conjecture. It may be that a temporary chapel was built on the present site, prior to the subsequent erection of the Congregational Church. There is no building shown on the 1867 Ordnance Survey, and the Minute Books of the period record the 'reopening' of the Church in 1874. During modern structural repairs to the Church, foundations have been uncovered indicating the existence of a building prior to the present one. Was this a smaller edifice, temporarily used for worship after the Iron Chapel had been vacated, or was the temporary use of the Iron Chapel extended until the new church was ready? We can only surmise.

There is much to record as the Congregational* Church grew into the 20th century and continued to develop. As with most denominations, there have been many trials and tribulations to negotiate, including two World Wars. The merger took place, in 1972, between the Congregational and Presbyterian Churches of England, to create the United Reformed Church. Both before and since, it has gained the reputation as a friendly and caring house of God, where the religious and social activities have been guided by a succession of very fine Ministers. The Winchmore Hill United Reformed Church has come a long way since that tiny wooden chapel was created at Wood Corner, nearly 250 years ago.

The western side of the Green was notable for two houses. The Limes stood facing the Green, near the junction with Broad Walk, and was demolished in 1955-56, when the maisonettes were built. I remember it being used as a headquarters of the British Red Cross Society during the last war. The Limes paled into insignificance alongside Uplands, which adjoined it.

Uplands was a very large residence indeed, dominated by tall

*The new name of Winchmore Hill Congregational Church was certified in December 1876.

42

The Old Independent Meeting

The seeds of the Congregational Church were sown here, at Wood Corner, in this tiny chapel.

The lovely back garden of Uplands. The Kings Head can just be seen, left, in the distance.

The fountain on the Green, looking west.

The changing scene on the Green.

chimney stacks, and the house and grounds spread right round into Church Hill. It was fronted by a dwarf wall plus a high hedge, and the rear elevation featured a large conservatory and beautiful gardens. It was the home of Dr. David Todd (1768-1839), Principal Surgeon to the Indian Civil Service, and his wife Frances (1787-1874). Frances, a widow for 35 years, was the gracious lady who earned the gratitude of the village when she paid for a pump to be installed on the Green in 1850. She also presented the altar and pulpit to St. Paul's Church, where there are tablets in her and her husband's memory.

Up to 1934, the entrance to Church Hill from the Green was very narrow, with only sufficient room for a footpath on the Kings Head side. When Uplands was demolished in that year and the block of flats was erected, the road was widened considerably.

The Kings Head was the old village inn, that bore no resemblance to the Kings Head and Railway Hotel, built in 1896 to replace it. The original inn was a simple, plain, two-storied house, Georgian in style and similar in character to the old Green Dragon, though wider in frontage. It faced on to Wades Hill with a tiny front garden, bordered by a picket fence, an ideal resting place for the upturned pewter tankards. It was a reddish-brown brick building, partially covered with wisteria, with a projecting portico supported by two imitation marble pillars. There was little to distinguish it from a private house, save a signboard above the coping and a lantern in front of the portico entrance.

The garden of the old inn was across the road, on the other side of Wades Hill, where the shops have since been built. There was a small pond here where the water lilies grew and all around was a profusion of flowers.

Once again, when the new public house was built, the road access into both Wades Hill and Church Hill was considerably widened. Some cottages in Church Hill were demolished, to make way for a fire station, forming an integral part of the pub. The two distinctive archways, offering suitably wide access, with their granite keepstones set for posterity, can still be seen, though the fire engines have long since departed. On the centre pier, near to ground level, we can identify an Ordnance Survey bench mark.

Next door was Devon House, which has recently been rebuilt causing the disappearance of the shop next door. Two arched openings have replaced it, similar in character to those of the old fire station. Devon House and the shop next door were, for many years, the domestic and trade premises of the local butcher, with home-killed meat a speciality. The slaughter house was originally in a covered yard at the side of the shop, but was later rebuilt at the rear. Langley, Gocher, Potter and Phillips were families who, in succession, ran the business.

Let us cross now to the eastern side of Wades Hill and proceed along the northern face of the Green. We notice a small external staircase, on the flank wall of the Post Office, leading up to the front door of, what used to be, the manager's private quarters above the shop. I still think of Paterson and Young's as I pass, though the premises are now Rochefort Antiques.

In the latter half of the 19th century, roughly where Westoby's and the adjacent shops are now situated, stood a most unusual long, low gabled cottage facing the Green. There were no foundations, for it stood on a framework of timber mounted on wheels which, in theory, made it a movable structure. The wheels had sunk to the axles and some lime trees had been planted in front, making the move impossible, even if it had been desirable. The cottage was subsequently demolished to make way for the shops. Miss Cresswell tells us of this early example of a movable home, a phenomenon usually associated with more modern times.

Many of the old shops have gone but, as we pass the newsagents and come to Elizabeth of the Green (No. 16, Downes' old shop), it is worthwhile pausing, for the next four shops have been built on to the face of the four old houses that once stood here. If we go into the florists, or Winchmore Antiques next door, we can see the steps at the rear of the shops, which led up to the original front doors of the houses, well set back from today's frontages. Elizabeth Bowen was most kind in taking me over the premises to explore the old house that has stood here from around 1827. One can identify the original front wall of the house at both ground and first floor levels, and, at the rear, the original black-tarred clapboarding is still intact.

The origins are similar in La Fondue where the ground floor level has to be reached by ascending some steps into the restaurant. This occupied the site of two of the old houses. Please observe the passageway, its entrance now guarded by a door, on the left hand side of the restaurant, which once led us to the blacksmith's shop, situated in a yard at the rear. It could also be approached from the Wilson Street end, and it was common practice for the horses to be led in to be shod, whilst the owners washed their carts in the village pond across the way. Although I have a 1933 photograph of the smithy, then looking very derelict, I believe it ceased to function in the 1920's, and has since been demolished.

Part of the restaurant site was once a private school which operated under the control of Miss Watkins, Miss Tebb and then Miss Tills, who was the daughter of Captain Tills of Fords Grove Cottage.

St. Paul's School in Church Hill was used for many of the early community meetings and concerts etc. but, in 1887, the Village Hall was erected to commemorate the jubilee of Queen Victoria. It stood facing the Green, at the junction with Wilson Street, on the site now occupied by shops. The hall was the social centre for the village and catered for a wide variety of activities but its life span was short. When St. Paul's Institute was built in 1903, thanks to the generosity of William Paulin and in memory of his wife Fanny, it was no longer needed and was then demolished.

Many of the shops have faded from the picture, after years of great service. Each one of you will have your own special memories of them so I will give just a few names to stimulate the mental processes. Paterson & Young's, Post Office and grocers, where Mr. Caplin was manager; Grout's, the drapers; Bolton's, the chemists; Salmon's, the plumbers; Nix's Dairy; Guy's, the newsagents; Downes', the corn merchants; Garrard's, the builders; John Buckle's, grocers and provisions etc.

There have been so many changes, with a marked tendency in recent decades for an influx of antique shops. The setting is right. In spite of everything, the area around the Green still retains a certain village atmosphere and a sense of history. Even the railway station nearby has changed little since 1871, when the first train went through. The biggest change of all, I suppose, is the saturation of traffic, but I have commented on this before and must refrain from repetition.

Wilson Street marks the line of the well-defined and ancient right of way, that has connected Middle Lane (Station Road) with Front Lane (Vicars Moor Lane) since time immemorial. It was known variously as the Trap Gates or the Clappers, which refers to the clap gates that featured along its way. The name clap gates still survives in some parts of the country, though they are now more commonly known as kissing gates. It reminds us of the origins of the name of Clappers Green, the hamlet and farm once situated at the top of Fox Lane. I have discussed this more fully in 'Once Upon a Time in Palmers Green'.

Wilson Street turns abruptly at right angles but, beyond the row of 19th century terraced houses, the footpath remains, running parallel to the railway and emerging on the western side of the bridge in Vicars Moor Lane.

We can glance at Moor Park House (2a Wilson Street), now a complex of flats, but once the site of Grove Lodge, the home of the Cresswell family for 22 years. Just downhill is Winchmore Hill Railway Station. I have written more on these matters in Chapter 5. On the southern side of Station Road, tight to the railway embankment, are the well-established King Easton Nurseries. Their strip of land runs by the side of the railway, right through to Compton Road.

To many of my readers, the house called Roseville will always be associated with Dr. Gordon and Mrs. Edith Simpson. The doctor tended my father when he became seriously ill in 1948, shortly after we moved to Seaforth Gardens, and he was also well-known to my wife's family.

Doctor Gordon Simpson will always be remembered for his great love of the outdoors and his strong, energetic and forthright personality. He was a great advocate of the Scout, Rover & Sea Cadet movements. Indeed, for a long period prior to World War II, Roseville was the H.Q. of No. 185 Scout Troop & Rover Crew. To all the youngsters he was affectionately known as 'Simbo', a man who was happy to spend his holidays in camp, sharing with them the delights of living under canvas. His wife Edith was a great support and was particularly interested herself in the Wolf Cub movement.

The doctor, son of Doctor Robert and Mrs. Louie Simpson, was born in Bristol. He was educated at Plymouth College but came to London Hospital to pursue his medical studies, where he qualified as house surgeon in 1916. He was commissioned as Lieutenant in the R.A.M.C. and in 1917, en route to India, his ship was torpedoed with 1500 on board. Many lives were lost.

In 1921, the family came to live at Roseville, with father and son in the practice together. His mother, Louie, was zealous in her interest in public life, and this continued with her work on the old Edmonton Board of Guardians. Gordon took over the practice and, at the wheel of his cherished open-top sports car, he became a familiar figure in the village. He married Edith in 1934 and they raised two sons, Peter and Andrew.

A keen Rotarian, the doctor was a man of strict principles and beliefs, supported by his unquestioned loyalty and kindness. His great delight, winter and summer, was to join the early morning regulars at Barrowell Green baths. He died in November 1956, aged 64, and is sadly missed by his family and friends, his patients, his

The lovely old shops on the Green remind us of the past.

The Green still retains its village atmosphere in this picture, though the traffic
'explosion' is still to come.

Today's picture of the Kings Head, rebuilt in 1896 to replace the old village inn. The arched openings of the fire station can still be identified and beyond is the refurbished Devon House.

The shops in 1989, with the Kings Head and Church Hill in the distance.

fellow Rotarians and, especially, his great chums in the many youth movements with which he was associated.

Mrs. Edith Simpson J.P. was born and educated in Scotland, but has given long and valuable service in public life in our locality, and continues to do so. In 1958-9, she was Mayoress to the Mayor of Southgate, Mrs. Ruth Winston Fox and, in 1988, she was given the Honorary Freedom of the London Borough of Enfield, 'in recognition of her outstanding contribution to the work of voluntary and charitable organisations in the Borough, for her long and valuable service to the administration of Justice and as an expression of the high esteem in which she is held.'

What do we know about Roseville's history? Roseville was thought to have been two houses originally, later converted into one. We know that the land came into the possession of John Decka in 1768 and that, shortly afterwards, he had the two houses built. The estate then exceeded 5 acres and included the site of the old St. Paul's Institute (now the District Sorting Office) in Station Road. In addition to the dwellings, stables, orchard and gardens, there were 4 acres of pasture land, including two large fields lying between Station Road and Compton Road. The railway was not to divide the estate until 1871.

In 1830, Roseville came into the hands of John Radford (already referred to in connection with the setting up of the Independent Church) and it remained with him and his heirs for 91 years. During that time, it was let to various tenants including John Ashley, Goods Manager of the Great Northern Railway. In 1879, Mr. Ashley had a large house called Vicarsmoor built, just beyond the bridge in Vicars Moor Lane, but he died before it was completed. The Company gave £1300 to his widow in recognition of his services, a sizeable sum in those days and indicative of the high regard in which he was held. The engraved stone 'J.A. 1879', was removed from the house when it was demolished in the 1960's, and let into the brick parapet of the bridge, where it can still be seen.

Prior to the Simpsons, from 1889 to 1921, Roseville was occupied by the Vivian family, well-known locally and also in the medical profession. Dr. R.T. Vivian and his wife, Annie, were the parents of three doctor sons, one of whom, Captain R.T. Vivian was killed in action in Mesopotamia in 1916, aged 27. There are brass tablets in St. Paul's Church to the memory of the doctor and his son, and a window in the Lady Chapel is dedicated to the memory of his wife, Annie, who died in 1939.

Annie was the daughter of the Sugdens of Oak Lodge, of whom I have written in my Southgate book. The Sugdens, too, had close connections with St. Paul's and there is a large window over the altar in the Lady Chapel in memory of Emma, wife of Samuel Sugden, who died in 1874.

Roseville was a rather plain ashlar-faced, flat-topped building of 3 storeys, relieved only by the entrance portico, which remains in my memory. This was a grand affair, with ornate capitals, enclosed by sidelight windows and half glass entrance doors. Roseville stood in a prestigious position, behind the brick boundary wall bordering the Green and was sheltered by mature trees and shrubs. For many years there was a large rookery in the grounds. One had a clearer view of the house through the wide entrance, situated near to the first of the adjacent three shops.

Roseville was demolished in the late fifties to make way for the flats we see there today. After nearly 200 years, we were witnessing the end of another chapter.

An apt phrase, perhaps, for we have travelled full circle now and are back to the three shops, built on the garden of the old village bakery. In 1929, these shops were occupied by Henry Davies (the butcher), John Volz (the watchmaker), and Wilfred F. Chalkley (the baker). Sixty years on, their modern counterparts are Quick Clean (launderette), Tumti (childrens clothes) and Clothes for Men.

In this chapter, we have sampled much of Winchmore Hill's history on our travels and have now returned to Hoppers Road, our starting point. I hope you have found the journey around the Green worthwhile and of interest, for it represents the very heart of the old village that has existed for centuries. Though the surroundings may have changed, that heart still beats today in the midst of surburbia.

# CHAPTER 4

## ALL ROADS LEAD TO THE KINGS HEAD

THE OLD VILLAGERS used to say – 'All roads lead uphill to the Kings Head' and, before Broad Walk was made up, it was a true and valid observation.

I wanted to include in this chapter all the roads that feed into the Green, the village centre as I call it, and to broaden its scope over a wide radius. You will realise that, by this ploy, I have licence to cover topics that have been difficult to include in other chapters. I have used the villagers' old saying for my chapter heading, simply dropping the word 'uphill'.

It has been difficult to devise a straightforward journey around Winchmore Hill but, hopefully, I have maintained a logical sequence. Hoppers Road and Broad Walk have been dealt with in other chapters and, continuing clockwise, we come to Church Hill.

Before St. Paul's was built in 1828 the road, which was little more than a track, was known as Chase Hill as far as the brook in the valley, near to the park entrance of today. Beyond, it was named Cock Hill, including the road now called Eversley Park Road. Winchmore Hill Road was once known as Chase Side. The entrances into Church Hill and Wades Hill, from the Green, were originally very narrow and restricted. We can still see today the curved wall in front of the Friends Meeting House, specifically built to allow the carriages to turn about in so restricted a road. When Uplands was demolished and the Kings Head was rebuilt, the opportunity was taken to widen these approaches.

We pass the Brethren's Meeting Room and arrive at the oldest religious foundation in the village. In 1988, the Society of Friends celebrated 300 years of Quakerism in Winchmore Hill. In fact, the story goes back before 1688.

The middle of the 17th century was a notable period for the setting up of dissenting sects, who were dissatisfied with the organised churches. Most of them have long since disappeared, but Quakerism has survived. George Fox founded the movement, when he discovered a new faith in 1647. 'I heard a voice', he said. In 1652, he preached on top of Pendle Hill in Lancashire to a large gathering. The Quaker movement was born and rapidly spread throughout England.

In 1662, a friend named William Brend held a meeting at

Thackers Yard, in a barn off Winchmore Hill Green. He had travelled widely, including to New England, where he had been thrown into prison and beaten for his Quaker beliefs. The meeting produced several converts to the new faith, and prompted many subsequent gatherings in the local houses and barns. The tiny hamlet of Winchmore Hill was becoming a small, but vital, centre for the Society of Friends.

In 1672, John and Elizabeth Oakley bought one acre of land off Church Hill, the site of the present grounds. John was a Merchant Tailor, a weaver and a silk merchant in the City, who had already been imprisoned for holding meetings at his house in Spitalfields. Now retired and undeterred, he and his wife came to live in Winchmore Hill, where they continued their illegal practices.

Life was far from easy for the Quakers in their formative years. They were hounded and persecuted for their beliefs, and treated as outcasts. In many ways, it was the very remoteness of our village that enabled a small band of faithfuls to survive, and encourage others from outside the district to join with them. Winchmore Hill was so isolated that such meetings were less likely to attract the attention of the authorities.

In 1682, the Oakleys gave the land and buildings to three Friends, on the understanding that they could continue to live in the house, rent free, until their death. John and Elizabeth died in 1684 and 1686 respectively, thus leaving the 'estate' in the hands of the Society. It was decided to build a new Meeting House, which was completed in 1688, when regular meetings commenced and the burial ground was officially opened.

George Fox was a regular visitor to Winchmore Hill and other local meetings. He made many friends here, including Elizabeth Dry of Enfield, Bridget Austell, who ran a girls' school in Southgate, and Edward Man of Fords Green in Winchmore Hill. I have spoken more of the latter in another chapter. George Fox set up the structure of worship in the Quaker faith with the Monthly, Quarterly and Yearly Meetings, which has remained to this day. His last visit to the Winchmore Hill Meeting was on 14th December 1690. He died one month later on 13th January 1691.

In 1700, it was estimated that there were 100,000 Quakers in the British Isles but, by 1800, because of the strict disciplines required, the number had dropped to 15,000.

The old Meeting House had reached the end of its useful life and, in 1790, it was demolished to make way for the present building. Some historians maintain that the old building was destroyed by fire, but this appears to be conjecture. Further building work was done in 1796, when the schoolroom and lobby were added and, in 1809, when the washroom (now the kitchen) was constructed.

Prominent persons in public life, and in the business world, gave the movement added prestige. These included Samuel Hoare (died 1796), the Barclay family of banking fame and John Fothergill M.D. (died 1780), an eminent physician who founded the Ackworth School in Yorkshire. At one time, the Walkers of Arnos Grove and the Bevans of Cockfosters gave their local support.

Burials continued at the rate of three to six a year and, by 1821, the upper part of the burial ground, near the road, was full and so the lower part, previously used for grazing, was opened. Because of poor drainage, burials ceased in 1980, by which time a total of 1,000 graves had been accommodated in the whole area.

The 20th century saw the growth of Winchmore Hill and an influx of middle class families into the district. The Meeting House was extensively renovated in 1911 and a cottage for the caretakers constructed in the grounds. This accommodation was extended in the 1970's, and further building work and refurbishment has taken place in recent years.

The story of the Quakers in Winchmore Hill reflects the strength of their quiet and simple faith that has endured and will continue.

Hill House was in Church Hill opposite Denleigh Gardens. I remember it well. It had a very austere exterior for it was a plain, square, flat-roofed building, yet it dated back to the days of Queen Anne (1702-14). It was built in front of, and attached to, two old cottages, thought to pre-date the house by some 200 years. The cottages became the kitchen and scullery arrangements for the house.

It was once the home of George Patten A.R.A., an acclaimed portrait painter of his day, whose subjects included Prince Albert, several of the City Fathers and the only portrait of Paganini. He died at Hill House in 1865, at the age of 64.

The Regnarts came to Hill House in 1878 and lived there until 1885, when Clare Henry Regnart J.P. purchased Stonehall nearby. He retained possession of his old home, however, letting it out to a succession of tenants and, on Clare's death in 1932, his son Horace moved back to Hill House and remained there until 1948, when he left for County Cork in Southern Ireland. It was there, in 1952, that Horace G. Regnart M.A. wrote his valuable book, that adds to our knowledge of the old village.

Great improvements were made to Hill House by the Regnarts. When 'C.H.' arrived, there was no gas, electricity or main drainage, and the well on the Green was the nearest source of water. Mr. Regnart altered all this and added a conservatory and tennis court. Hill House was demolished in 1960 and the name has been preserved in the Close nearby, where some modern town houses have been built.

A little further down the hill, nearly opposite St. Paul's Church, there was a long low house with a verandah. It was surrounded by gardens and open fields, stretching down to the brook in the valley. This was the home of Mr. Truscott, who became Alderman Sir Francis Wyatt Truscott and was Lord Mayor of London 1879-80. Before the railway arrived in the village in 1871, Sir Francis walked daily to and from Wood Green station. In those days, this would not have been considered unusual, as people were accustomed to walking long distances as a matter of course. Sir George, son of Francis, likewise served as Lord Mayor in 1908-09.

The house was demolished in 1881 and Laurel Lodge was built on the site by Thomas Mann for his son Edward (later Sir Edward Mann). When his mother died in the 1890's, Sir Edward moved to Roseneath and Laurel Lodge became the home of Fred Barry, son of Mr. Barry of Bush Hill House, grandson of the architect, Sir Charles Barry, and nephew of the civil engineer, Sir John Wolfe Barry. Fred was followed by Mr. Charles Morgan, once of Grove Lodge, who lived there until his death in 1909. Later known as The Laurels, many of us will remember it as The Chesterfield Club in the 1950's prior to subsequent demolition.

In 1872, the mansion of Stonehall was built in those open fields I have mentioned. Opposite, and just down from the church, we can still see the lodge with the date engraved on its plaque. Stonehall was built to the order of Mr. Alfred Walker, proprietor of Stone's, makers of British wines. There were so many of his namesakes living in the area at the time and, to make identification clear, he was always referred to as 'Ginger Wine' Walker, for obvious reasons. Alfred Walker was a successful candidate in the first election of the Southgate Local Board, after the separation from Edmonton in 1881.

The actual builder of Stonehall was Mr. Palmer, whose other activities included serving as licensee of the Kings Head nearby. Much of the building material used was salvaged from Beaver Hall, which had been demolished in 1870. This included the main staircase, the doors and the windows. I have written in detail about Beaver Hall in my book on Southgate. The mansion, home of the

This picture shows the once narrow entry into Church Hill, with Uplands boundary wall on the left, and the Kings Head and Devon House on the right.

A closer view of the old Devon House and the butcher's premises beyond.

The Friends Meeting House, the oldest religious foundation in the village.

*(right)*
St. Paul's Church.

58

Schneider family, stood in beautiful grounds just off Waterfall Lane, where Chandos Avenue lies today. It says much for the quality of the joinery of those days that it justified re-use in a house of Stonehall's calibre.

The stones of the old Blackfriars Bridge were used in the foundations and also in the construction of the cellar walls of the new building. Henrietta Cresswell tells us that a lady (not named) bought the massive stones in the late 1860's, when the old bridge was demolished, and had them transported to Winchmore Hill, where they lay neglected in a field off Wades Hill for some years. This must have been a costly exercise, scarcely justified by their ultimate fate.

When C.H. Regnart purchased Stonehall, in 1885, he carried out a vast range of improvements. It looks a lovely stately home in the photographs. The house was clad in greenery with a semi-circular entrance drive and lawn in front. Adjoining the main building, Regnart had extensive upper and lower conservatories constructed. He had rooms formed in the roof and built a dairy at the rear. There was excellent pasture, which provided grazing for a large herd of Jerseys. He enlarged the carriage house and stables, and added several outbuildings at the far end of a large kitchen garden. It had become a successful, productive dairy farm.

On C.H. Regnart's death in 1932, and the return of his son to Hill House, the estate was sold up for development. Stonehall was demolished and the cellars filled in. The stones of old Blackfriars Bridge have found their permanent resting place beneath the gardens of suburbia.

The villagers of Southgate had long been accustomed to the walk to All Saints in Edmonton, their religious centre for centuries. The building of the Weld Chapel, in 1615, had eased the situation but, as the hamlets grew into villages, it became clear that a more significant and local house of worship was needed. Christ Church duly arrived in 1862 and I have told this story elsewhere. The villagers of Winchmore Hill, too, had trod the path to All Saints for centuries. Their needs were duly recognised by the building of St. Paul's Church which was consecrated as a chapel of ease to All Saints in 1828 by the Rev. William Howley, Bishop of London, later to become Archbishop of Canterbury.

As with Christ Church, the wealthy landowners played their part in helping the scheme on its way. The site was donated by Mr. Walker Gray of Southgate Grove (later to become Grovelands), and various benefactors, including the Curries of Bush Hill House, donated sums to assist the Church Building Commissioners with the cost of construction.

St. Paul's is known as one of the 'Waterloo' churches, built to provide for the urban overspill following the Napoleonic Wars and, at a time of financial constraint, the architecture is often described as functional or 'Churchwardens Gothic'. The rather plain, simple style of the exterior remains much as it was nearly 160 years ago. Photographs taken in 1912 show the church to be completely clad in ivy, but this has disappeared. There have been many changes internally. In 1844, some thieves broke in and accidentally set fire to the east end of the church, which was badly damaged and required reinstatement.

St. Paul's became a separate Parish in 1851, since when it has continued to serve an important role in the religious and social life of the village.

In 1859, the Winchmore Hill National School, later to be known as St. Paul's Church of England School, was built on land donated by Mr. Walker Gray's successor at Grovelands, Mr. John Donnithorne Taylor. A grand concert was held to announce the opening. It was a quaint building, resembling a small church or chapel, with its own clock and tower facing the road. I remember it well and so does my wife, one of its pupils. Many residents will, no doubt, have their own personal recollections of life in the classroom there.

By 1958, the building was deemed to be unsafe and, after a temporary stay in St. Paul's Institute, the school moved to its present site in Ringwood Way in 1961, where it was opened by H.R.H. the Princess Alexandra. St. Paul's Church of England Primary School maintains a high reputation today, and the buildings and the facilities have been much improved over the years.

The Paulin family of Broadfields in Wades Hill were great benefactors to the local community and were especially supportive of St. Paul's. In 1903, William (later Sir William) Paulin erected St. Paul's Institute in memory of his wife, Fanny. Ten years later, after the marriage of his daughter, Ina, to the Rev. A.J.B. Dewdney of St. Paul's, he donated the land on which the Vicarage was to be built next to the Church. Sadly by this time, because of ill health and on doctor's orders, the Minister and his family had emigrated to Canada.

Although it was a very popular venue, the old Institute in Station Road was not an easy building to maintain economically and, after the demolition of the school buildings next to the church, a new parish hall and car park were built on the site and opened in 1966.

Subsequently, St. Paul's Institute was demolished and the site is now occupied by a G.P.O. District Sorting Office.

And so we progress down Church Hill. The road is narrow and still winds its way into the valley. We pass by three cottages on our left that belong to another time. The middle one, 'The Old School House, c1785', is of special interest, for it was the village school until 1859, when the National School was opened at St. Paul's. We wonder just how many pupils have climbed those steps that lead up to its entrance and listened to their teacher's words of wisdom in the tiny classroom.

Winchmore Hill then was a remote country village, free from noise and bustle. Life was much simpler, and lived at a much slower pace. There were no cars, aeroplanes, telephones, electricity, radio or television. The railway was yet to arrive. Our means of conveyance was provided by the horse or, more often, we walked. How quickly the transformation has come!

Before we leave Church Hill, perhaps we should stand amongst the trees below The Spinney and look up the hill from whence we came, with the cottages on our right and St. Paul's Church just visible in the distance. We look to our right to see the park entrance across the way and, beyond the dip in the road, is a rather updated Chase Side Tavern. If we ignore the modern houses and blot out the traffic from our senses, we can still find time to stand and stare, as we recall those peaceful days of yore, when man and nature seemed in perfect harmony.

We pass the entrance to Grovelands, once the home estate of the Taylors, and proceed beyond the dip in the road, towards the Chase Side Tavern. Years ago, there were two more farms on our right, the Model Farm, latterly associated with the Merrell family, and another smaller farm kept by Tom Nickels. Once again, we are reminded of the important part farming played in the livelihood of our community. The Model Farm later became a private residence and was renamed Camelot. It was a pretty house on the hillside but, according to Miss Cresswell, an unlucky one, where several aspiring farmers had hoped to make their fortunes but, in reality, had struggled to make a living.

Some fine houses were built on this side of the road in the late 1800's, some of which have been demolished in recent years, to make way for flats. There was also development at the extreme western end of Houndsden Road, where a little cul-de-sac was formed, that led on to the footpath, taking us across to Wades Hill.

The cul-de-sac was then known as Eversley Road.

The road frontages of the Church Hill/Winchmore Hill Road corner were fringed with beautiful mature trees, marking the edge of the Grovelands estate. Well into this century, Winchmore Hill Road remained a country lane, with not a single house on the south side, except for Hope House, said to be the dower house of the Taylors. This was a late 18th century farmhouse, with its own gardens and land, that is thought to pre-date Grovelands, the mansion that Walker Gray had built in 1797, which he called Southgate Grove.

The photographs I have of the Chase Side Tavern tell their own story. The original inn was Georgian, very similar in character to the original Kings Head on the Green or the original Fox at the bottom of Fox Lane. We see a plain, two-storied building with a familiar portico and 'marbled' pillar supports marking the entrance, above which some troughs of flowers help to relieve its rather stark appearance. The brewers name board (Mann, Crossman & Paulin) can be seen at parapet level. The old inn was demolished around 1902 to make way for a new, much grander, establishment.

Once again, we can detect the building fashions of the period. The new public house was more like an hotel with a large, hanging lantern on the corner and, at roof level, a tower surmounted with a cupola. One can detect similarities with today's Kings Head (built in 1896) and the Fox (built in 1904). However, the second Chase Side Tavern has not endured for, in 1937, a third version was built, again reflecting the style and fashion of the period. On this occasion, the opportunity was taken to set the building back further, to allow easier access into Eversley Park Road.

Legend maintains that a gibbet (or gallows) once stood near the old tavern and thus the road came to be known as Cock Hill. The story is quoted from several sources but it took me some time to follow the reasoning. For gallows, read gallus which is an old English form of the word gallows and is also Latin for cock*. The modern name of the road is, of course, derived from the Eversley Park estate that it bordered. Eversley Mount and Gallus Close are names of more recent developments that remind us of the past.

Just downhill from the tavern was Carter Page's nursery and the home of the original Carter Page. He fought in the Crimean War and came home to start a nursery in Winchmore Hill. His business

*The logic seems somewhat obscure, yet I have heard of a similar theory put forward on the naming of the old Cock Inn (Manhattan) at Bowes Road. It does appear that our old inns and taverns were favoured sites for the gibbets to be erected.

Hill House was once the home of George Patten A.R.A.,
before Clare Henry Regnart took possession in 1878.

Stonehall was built to the order of Alfred 'Ginger Wine' Walker,
before the Regnarts took possession in 1885.

A delightful scene in Church Hill where the old Schoolhouse c1785 still remains.

Church Hill of another era when we could walk in the roadway,
for there was so little traffic.

grew and his nurseries multiplied. He opened a shop in the City where he sold some of his produce, and his name became well-known in the field of horticulture. His two sons, Thomas and Charles Page, continued the business.

We climb the hill and approach the Chaseville Park estate, a pleasant area with its own shopping parade. Just into Worlds End Lane is the entrance to Highlands Hospital. This was built in 1886 by the Metropolitan Asylums Board, the statutory authority then responsible for asylums and fever hospitals. The decision to build the hospital is said to have delayed the development of the Chaseville Park estate for many years, due to local fears that the area could become contaminated by germs from the hapless patients.

It was originally called the Northern Hospital and was used for fever and convalescent cases, especially for children, who could recover in the clean country air which was then readily available. The horse ambulances were a familiar sight in the locality in those days. Built on a site of 36½ acres, there were 19 separate pavilions built around a pear shaped loop of service road, accommodating in all nearly 800 beds.

Like its neighbour South Lodge, which opened as Enfield Isolation Hospital in 1900, Highlands has adapted to requirements over the years. In 1913, 4 pavilions were allocated to patients suffering from tuberculosis, and its role as a fever and convalescent hospital gradually diminished. In 1948, it was grouped together with the Royal Northern Hospital, and a new title, Highlands, became necessary to avoid confusion. It had become the District General Hospital and, in 1966, was merged with South Lodge.

The future of Highlands, however, is very precarious to say the least. It appears that Chase Farm Hospital on the Ridgeway is being developed and increased, both in size and scope, to make way for Highlands' closure.

The team of consultants and surgeons, not forgetting the nursing staff and all connected with the hospital's administration, have done a tremendous job over the years. Highlands will be sadly missed.

The boundaries of the Eversley Park estate are formed today by Eversley Park Road, Green Dragon Lane, Wades Hill and Hounsden Gutter. This is being over generous, because the southern boundary was formed, in part, by a footpath which ran to the north of the stream at the Wades Hill end. However, it may help us to visualise the extent.

The main entrance was at the top of Wades Hill, where the lodge still stands, with a second entrance in Eversley Park Road (about 50 yards down from the bend in the road). The stables were in Green Dragon Lane. Years ago, the scene in this area was one of tree-lined lanes with ditches either side, and the beeches and oaks meeting overhead in a canopy of green.

The site of the mansion, near the western segment of Eversley Crescent, had been a gravel pit and an area of rabbit warren. A Mr. Wigan had the mansion built by Cubitts in 1865, with a well, sunk to a depth of 350 feet, to provide fresh water. This was one of the deepest wells in the locality.

Photographs show Eversley to be a large, solidly built, Victorian mansion with tall chimney stacks and a central tower. The entrance was approached by climbing steps into an unusual, tunnel-like porch. The building looks set to last forever, and the heart mourns that all that skill and workmanship, coupled with some of the finest building materials available, endured for little over 50 years.

Mr. Wigan lived there with his wife until 1884, when it remained empty for some years. Eventually Caroline, Marchioness of Ely, took up the tenancy. She was often seen being driven about the district in her carriage and pair. She had particularly fine, high-stepping bay horses with black manes, kept in the peak of condition and always immaculately groomed, with ear-knots of crimson satin ribbon tied into their bridles. The Marchioness died at Eversley in 1917.

The Wigans decided to sell the Eversley Park estate for development and Westoby's board went up by the lodge, indicating that the whole 38 acre site was on offer. The development duly went ahead with Eversley Crescent being constructed in 1922.

Wades Hill is one of the old roads of the village, named after John Wade of Beaumont Lodge. More about that in a moment. I have already written about the Kings Head and explained that the shops opposite now occupy the ground once taken up by the gardens of the inn.

Things change so quickly these days. Until recent times, Wades Mews gave us access to the Dairy, and the shops on either side, that I remember so well, are but a memory. The first premise (No. 1) was Aldridge's, the greengrocer, though it had previously been Lovelace's, the shoe shop, and next door was Marlow's, the sweet shop, so well remembered by this scribe. Many of my readers will recall Tancock's, the florists. The shop was originally part of what is now 17 Wades Hill, where the Tancocks lived. In later years the shop moved further along Wades Hill, nearer to the Green. The end shop is now a restaurant but, for most of its life, has served as a fishmongers – Strangwick's to my generation. Mrs. Strangwick still lives in the locality.

I have a photograph of the shop, taken before the First World War when it was owned by Mr. Weeks. His pre-Christmas poultry display is most impressive, with enough birds to satisfy the whole village it seems. Likewise, I have seen many photographs of the old butchers' shops, with large carcasses of meat hung in abundance, on open display, to the great delight of a very proud shopkeeper. Today, I imagine, the Public Health Inspector would not be too impressed.

Beyond the shops, on the eastern side of Wades Hill, are some of the older dwellings including four clapboarded cottages which have been well preserved.

At the turn of the century, on the western side of Wades Hill, extending from the Kings Head down to Glenwood House, were Braid's Nurseries. There were several greenhouses, and a thick well-trimmed holly hedge lined the roadway. Mr. Braid, a kindly Scot, was renowned for his pelargoniums, in summer, and Chinese primroses and cinerarias, in winter and early spring. His reputation had spread far and wide, yet he was always willing to assist the locals with plants for their cottage gardens at giveaway prices. The nurseries gave way to development with more shops, some housing and the formation of Wades Grove.

I well remember Mr. Knowles' cycle shop, on the corner with Wades Grove, and a small ladies hairdressers called Glama. My family knew Gladys and Marjorie, the young ladies who founded the business and whose combined names formed its title.

Opposite Barber Close stands Glenwood House, a tall, rather austere looking, 18th century residence of 4 storeys, which includes a mansard roof and dormers. It served as a vicarage for St. Paul's Church for a time during the last century and has also been used as a private school. Glenwood House was one of a pair, as there was an even larger residence adjoining called The Elms, which had extensive grounds at the rear. This was demolished in 1935, but here we should pause for a moment.

In 1929, Miss A.C. Harper started Keble Preparatory School when, encouraged by the parents of boys who met her at Palmers Green High School, where she was a teacher, she admitted 5 boys and 2 girls to a class at St. John's Church Hall. In 1930, they moved to The Elms, a large house set in a beautiful garden in Wades Hill.

A year later, Miss S. Swinburne joined the staff and the number of pupils steadily climbed. In 1935, the present school was built in the grounds and the old house demolished. The story has been one of continued expansion and improved facilities over the years.

By the outbreak of war, when Keble was evacuated, there were 100 pupils in attendance, and the numbers now exceed 200. Miss Swinburne duly became Headmistress in 1955, and retired from the post in 1971, 40 years after joining the staff. She helped to turn the school into an Educational Trust in 1968, run by a Board of Governors as a charity. Today, Keble maintains its high reputation as a first class Kindergarten and Preparatory School for boys up to the age of 13. I am most grateful to Mrs. Lacey, the secretary, and to Miss Swinburne, for their willing assistance with my research.

Just beyond the school entrance is Harwoods Yard where, tucked away off the beaten track, we can discover a small group of 19th century houses hidden from the road. There is no way through but one kind lady let me into her back garden, where the rear wall of the garage complex can be seen, with the tablet and date inscribed, 1877 (the year of William Paulin's marriage). This is part of the old stables that once belonged to the Broadfields estate. I visited the garage and, with permission, investigated further, climbing the rickety stairs to the hayloft, now filled with tyres and motor accessories.

Broadfields was the home of the Paulins and I have written more about this great family, their kindness and their influence on village life, on many pages throughout this book.

William Thomas Paulin, son of Thomas, was 17 when the family moved from Stoke Newington to come and live at Beaulieu in Winchmore Hill. Having previously acquired the Broadfields estate of 14 acres, he married Fanny Mann at Christ Church Southgate in 1877, thus uniting two of the great brewery families, already linked in business. A small farm had stood here in the open countryside, prior to William building his new family home. The old farm is clearly marked on the 1st edition (1867) O.S. Map, as is Broadfields on the 2nd edition (1897).

The entrance drive to Broadfields, which was roughly on the line of Paulin Drive, terminated in a circular loop in front of the house which, according to my calculations, stood some 120 yards back from Wades Hill, i.e. where Broadfields Avenue runs today. The Paulins kept a fine herd of Jerseys, which were a most popular breed of cows in the locality at this time. You may remember, from my Southgate book, that Doctor Corner favoured them, as their milk

The Chase Side Tavern through the ages.

Highlands Hospital has served since 1886, but its future seems uncertain.

Eversley, the home of Caroline, Marchioness of Ely.

was relatively free of the bacillus that caused tuberculosis.

The marriage of William and Fanny was the key to a most productive and happy partnership, which blossomed as Winchmore Hill began to grow from a hamlet into a village. The Paulins were a very wealthy family but their generosity to the village, in monetary terms, is only a small part of the story. Their love for the village and its people, and their desire to help in a wide variety of ways to those less fortunate, was soon apparent. They came to be known as Lord and Lady Bountiful of Winchmore Hill and, after Fanny's untimely death in 1901 at the age of 49, her younger daughter, Irene, took over the role with renewed and untiring devotion.

The eldest daughter, Ina, married the Rev. A.J.B. Dewdney of St. Paul's in 1902 and was able to play an active part in local affairs until 1907. At this time, the parish was saddened to hear that the Minister, having contracted tuberculosis, felt compelled to resign. On medical advice, after a stay in Switzerland, the family, which included their baby daughter, emigrated to Canada.*

Sir William T. Paulin J.P. was awarded his knighthood in 1929, chiefly in recognition of his work for the London Hospital, where he had been a Life Governor for over half a century. I have touched on his benevolence in local matters in other chapters, especially with regard to St. Paul's, the Winchmore Hill Cricket Club and the setting up of Roseneath in Vicars Moor Lane as a fully equipped hospital. There are many other kindnesses left unrecorded.

We pass by the garage I always knew as Broadfields Garage (now Ironside Motors Ltd) and, on the other side of Paulin Drive, are the Esther Doe Almshouses. These were originally erected in 1868 for '12 spinsters of limited means and incapable of earning a living'. They were financed by Esther Doe in memory of her husband Joseph Bolton Doe, ironfounder of Whitechapel, Middlesex and Brixton Hill, Surrey and her father Richard Harman, silk manufacturer of Bethnal Green, Middlesex and North Brixton, Surrey. Many of us will remember the old houses (Memorial Row), demolished in 1974 to make way for the new.

As we pause awhile and look to the north we can clearly see the lofty spire of St. Mary Magdalene, built in 1883 at the top of Windmill Hill. It still remains a great landmark for miles around. To the north of Vicars Moor Lane, Wades Hill was a lovely, winding country lane right up until the early 1930's, when development began in earnest with the straightening of the road. Photographs as

*The Reverend A.J.B. Dewdney became Archdeacon of Calgary and died in 1946.

71

late as 1928 and 1929, taken down the hill from the village end, show a grass-covered lane with two-wheeled tracks worn down to the gravel, surrounded by open fields, dotted with beautiful mature trees.

There are no pavements and only two lamp posts in evidence. One of these stands opposite Vicars Moor Lane, the only side road off the hill, and the other in the dip, where two small rails guard the brook on either side. Of course, roundabouts had not even been thought of then, and Houndsden Road and Hadley Way did not exist. There were, however, some delightful walks. One entered a kissing gate, just on the north side of the stream known as Hounsden* Gutter, and walked through a field and over a stile into a tiny narrow lane, that would lead us on to the old Chase Side Tavern. Where better to pause for refreshment on a hot summer's day? This charming rural scene could be enjoyed right up to 1930, when the demolition of Percy Lodge and Avondale College triggered off the housing development that was to come.

The Broadfields and Roseneath estates were put up for sale in 1931. It was another major turning point. Many parts of the estate were purchased by the Ingram family, highly reputable builders in the area. More of that later. The whole character of the area was soon to undergo a rapid transformation. When one looks at the same scene in the photograph of 1933, taken from the same spot, it is difficult to believe we are in the same locality. The open fields, the trees and the winding country lane have all disappeared under bricks and mortar. It is almost unbelievable.

Wades Hill was named after John Wade, a retired merchant tailor, who came to live at Beaumont Lodge, situated on the northern corner with Vicars Moor Lane. It was a very large, three-storied, 'L' shaped house, covered with greenery and bounded by a high brick wall, which extended up the hill and returned along Vicars Moor Lane. John Wade was a very wealthy man, who owned a great deal of farmland in the area, most of which was given over to rich pasture for his livestock. Attractive lawns, flower gardens and orchards surrounded the immediate vicinity of Beaumont Lodge.

I have read so much about all the wealthy landowners who lived in our area in years gone by. I have tried to assess their characters and their motives through the observations of others. Almost without exception, there has been nothing but praise for their

*All the old maps spell it thus, though Houndsden Road, for some reason, has acquired an extra 'd'.

contribution towards community life, their commitment to help others less fortunate, their love of the area in which they lived and the people they employed, their generosity of spirit as well as their charity.

It came as a surprise, therefore, to read in Regnart's book of the recollections of Harry Cox, an old villager, whose father was bailiff of Mr. Wade's estate. The Wades are described as being 'very pompous' and said to be held in ridicule because 'they were not real gentry'. There was other criticism, too, that we should not heed unduly, but it was so unexpected, that it struck a note of discord.

John Wade died in 1865. His lovely house became the Avondale College for Girls, which soon gained a fine reputation. It was a high class establishment, kept latterly by Miss Steele until its demise in 1929.

On the opposite corner with Vicars Moor Lane stood Percy Lodge, once the home of Sharon Turner (1768-1847). He was a noted historian and close friend of Isaac Disraeli, father of Benjamin. Turner wrote several books and arranged for Benjamin Disraeli's admission into the Church of England.

Percy Lodge was also the home of the Schofield family for more than 30 years. Mr. Charles Schofield was the first man to ride a velocipede in Winchmore Hill in the early 1860's. Miss Cresswell describes it as a 'cumbrous vehicle upon four wooden wheels'. Her father, Dr. John Cresswell, used a tricycle extensively on his rounds, whilst brother Frank favoured the 'Ordinary' (penny-farthing) for cycle rides with his friends. Many inventors tried their hand at the development of the bicycle, which became very popular in the 1880's and 1890's. The 'Boneshaker' and the 'Ordinary' are perhaps best remembered, before the introduction of the safety bicycle and pneumatic tyres.

Avondale College and Percy Lodge are just a memory now. Their disappearance in 1930, coupled with the sale of Sir William Paulin's estates, marked the end of an era.

As we climb Wades Hill at its northern end, we approach the lodge (now a private residence) to the old Eversley Park estate. However, before we reach there, we should contemplate the land within the triangle formed by Wades Hill, Green Dragon Lane and Hounsden Gutter. This was once the rich farmland of 'The Chase', comprising some 14 acres.

The farm could be entered via a longish drive from Wades Hill, or a much shorter approach from Old Green Dragon Lane. The 'Old' is clearly marked on the 1st edition of Ordnance Survey. It simply indicates that it was the lane that once led to the *old* Green Dragon Inn, which was situated originally at Masons Corner, before the removal to its present site (see Chapter 6). Nearly opposite to 'The Chase' was Filcap's Farm, the entry being where Landra Gardens is today. Once again, we are reminded that farming was the basic occupation and our means of existence, less than a century ago.

Vicars Moor Lane is an interesting road to explore today, for there is such a wide variety of dwellings, from the very old to the very new, to see and compare.

I have mentioned elsewhere the tiny chapel, now a private residence, where the Udallites and the Strict Baptists once worshipped. Just west of this was Beadle's furniture and upholstery shop, a large-fronted premise where Regnart remembers the rolls of oilcloth propped up against the outside wall. There was a bad fire in 1880 which gutted the place. Mr. Beadle never rebuilt the shop or resumed business. Instead, he built the three fine houses now numbered 108, 110 and 112 on the site of his burnt out premises and he continued to live opposite in Herbert Lodge, which was demolished for road widening in 1905.

As we approach the railway bridge, there are some delightful old cottages on our left, though three fell victim to the coming of the railway in 1871, to make way for the 'iron road'. These stood well back from the road, with pretty gardens at front and back. Mrs. Cresswell, mother of the doctor, lived in the cottage at the eastern end, which was remembered so poignantly by her grand-daughter 'Winifred' (her pet name for Henrietta). I have written of this elsewhere.

The great demand for building land in the suburbs has resulted in every conceivable space being considered for development. This has included areas adjacent to the railway tracks, previously deemed to be unsuitable. There are many such examples locally, and here the old coal and goods yard has been swallowed up by a new road (Stratfield Park Close) and housing on the western side of the bridge.

We cross the railway bridge and see the old yew tree growing in the back garden of 'Inver'. This is the first of an elegant row of fine houses, featuring entrance porticos, built in the second half of the 19th century. Just beyond, but much further back from the lane, with a semi-circular entrance drive, once stood Surburban House, marked as Prospect House on some of the old maps. It stood in extensive grounds and the owners acted as landlords, drawing rents

Beaumount Lodge, once the home of John Wade,
became the Avondale College for Girls.

Wades Hill, looking south, in 1929.
It was then just a track through open countryside.

Wades Hill, looking north, in 1929.

The same view in 1933. Just compare the two photographs
to witness a transformation.

from the tenants of several properties built nearby.

It was the home of two brothers, Charles and William Brett, who had made their money as hardware merchants in Birmingham. They were strict Quakers, even to the extent of wearing the Quaker style of dress at all times. They both left their money to their cook, who set up home there and married a Mr. Arlow (not related to the Arlows of Highfield Park). Mr. Arlow, a quiet, retiring character, died in 1910, leaving most of a considerable estate to his second wife, a kind lady who gave freely to several good causes in the village.

Surburban House and its ground came on the market in 1925 and development ensued, including the construction of Hoodcote Gardens and Green Moor Link. The names remind us of Thomas Hood's connection with this area and the joining of *Green* Dragon Lane and Vicars *Moor* Lane.

On the south side of the lane, close to the railway, stood Vicarsmoor, a large house built by John Ashley in 1879, of which I have written in the previous chapter.

Slightly to the east, on the same side of the lane, stood the Roseneath estate. I have written about Roseneath in Chapter 8, because the Mann family, who lived here, were closely connected with cricket at local and higher levels. Their history is entwined with Winchmore Hill Cricket Club and the Paulins, both in family and business matters.

It was in 1871, that the first Winchmore Hill Village Cricket and Lawn Tennis Club was established at Roseneath by Thomas Mann. It was an elite club and the sport was played in the most beautiful surroundings on the Roseneath estate. Dr. W.G. Grace is thought to have played here on more than one occasion. It was nine years later (1880) that a cricket club was established at the Fords Grove headquarters, which has endured to the present day.

I have photographs of Roseneath showing it to be an elegant residence, with the finest lawns and gardens, surrounded by an estate of 14 acres. Like Grovelands, Roseneath became a hospital for wounded soldiers during the First World War, thanks to the generosity of the owner, William (later Sir William) Thomas Paulin. It was thereafter used as a private nursing home.

Following Sir William's death, his estates were put up for auction in October 1931. They included Roseneath and Broadfields, and other property, divided into lots and totalling some 36 acres. All the larger lots were bought by the Ingram family who were builders of high repute in the area.

Arthur, father of George Ingram purchased Broadfields and the construction of Broadfields Avenue, Paulin Drive and Cresswell Way resulted. George bought the Roseneath estates including Rose Cottage and other property in Vicars Moor Lane. The house at Roseneath was demolished in 1936. The Council's original intention was to extend Radcliffe Road to link Station Road with Vicars Moor Lane. In the event, Mr. Ingram built Ringwood Way as it now stands. He was considering retiring from the building trade at the time and decided to retain ownership of most of these houses and let them as an investment.

The name Ringwood Way arose when the borough surveyor was seeking a name for the new road. Knowing George Ingram was a keen fisherman, he enquired where he did most of his fishing. 'In Hampshire, down Ringwood way' was the answer and so the road was christened.

An area of land off Radcliffe Road remained enclosed and difficult to develop. In the 1920's, a bowling club had been formed from those using the municipal green in Grovelands Park. In 1932, a number of its members, including Mr. E.J. Westoby, approached George Ingram about a possible home for a new Winchmore Hill Bowling Club. The rest, as they say, is history.

As we approach the corner with Ringwood Way, we should stop and look at No. 59, for this was the site of Rose Cottage and a plaque on the wall provides more information. Thomas Hood (1799-1845) was a poet and humorist of Scottish descent, who made full use of the pun. He lived with his family in Winchmore Hill for 3 years, from 1828 to 1831. Rose Cottage in Vicars Moor Lane was his home and one of his daughters, Frances, was born there in 1830.

It was a delightful Georgian house, that was added to in later years, and was surrounded by lawns and flower beds. A brick wall and a border of trees lined the roadway, ensuring privacy. Tom Hood's greatest friend was Charles Lamb, which probably influenced his move to the locality, for he was a frequent visitor to the Lambs' household in Enfield.

One of Hood's poems 'Our Village' is thought to refer to Winchmore Hill, for it paints an accurate picture of the Green as it appeared 160 years ago.

Following a disagreement with his landlord on the subject of repairs, Hood left Winchmore Hill to live at Lake House in Wanstead, a step he was later to regret for, it is reported, he sadly missed his old home.

Rose Cottage was subsequently the home of the Warners, who

moved from The Shrubbery. They were followed by the Rev. A.C. Drought, vicar of St. Paul's, and then Julia Mann, sister of Fanny. The house was demolished following bomb damage during the Second World War.

The Hagfields Footpath is lost forever, but is worth recalling. It linked Vicars Moor Lane with Green Dragon Lane (once called Dog Kennel Lane), and ran roughly on the line of what is Green Moor Link today. There were five stiles to negotiate in such a short distance and the footpath was very secluded, being shrouded by trees and shrubs on either side. The path was said to be haunted by an old hag and had no illumination. Many of the villagers would not use it after dark.

Near the Green Dragon Lane end stood The Retreat, a very ancient hostelry, best described as a beerhouse, where the farm and market garden labourers would adjourn for their morning and afternoon breaks. The landlord's name was Pomfret.

Fortunately Doctor Cresswell recorded the spot, from several different aspects, in his sketches and watercolours, which gave us a very clear impression of the inn and the surrounding countryside, as it was around 1865-70. One viewpoint was from Green Dragon Lane, say 100 yards west of Old Park Ridings, looking towards Green Lanes. We travel back in time, 120 years from now. Green Dragon Lane is no more than a rough track. Tall trees shade the lane and some stray cows graze contentedly by the wayside. In the distance we see The Retreat, near the corner where the footpath enters and, in the foreground, is an old shed – Pomfret's Pigsties. The scene is of another age, another world.

Another view has been sketched from the footpath, looking north, and we see the inn more clearly. It is no more than a clapboarded cottage, adapted for its purpose. Beyond is the beautiful countryside of open fields and orchards belonging to Old Park Grange, latterly known as Pike's Farm. We can pick out the white farmhouse in the distance, which lay by the footpath, near the top of the hill. We know it as Old Park Ridings today. This charming walk to Enfield remained a favourite with the villagers until after the turn of the century. What a delight it must have been!

The first edition (1867) O.S. Map shows two dwellings on the southern side of Vicars Moor Lane, very near to its junction with Green Lanes, and just one house of some stature, Drayton Villa, on the northern side. These apart, the whole scene from Roseneath to the Green Dragon was of unspoilt countryside.

Drayton Villa stood 100 yards from the inn, i.e. some 30 or 40 yards east of where Drayton Gardens joins today. The Villa was set back from the lane with a small farmyard and buildings at the rear. It was the home of the Booth family for many years, the owner being the founder of the world famous gin, to which he gave his name.

Almost opposite, but just up the hill, was the source of another liquid, equally precious. This was the Vicar's Well, sunk early in the 18th century by a Vicar of Edmonton, for the use of his parishioners over a wide radius. Hescott Terrace and Pritchett Terrace (1877) were built 150 years later, but the well's location can best be identified today by inspecting the gulley in the forecourt of the garage attached to 41, Vicars Moor Lane. Where the fresh clean water was once drawn, the rainwater now disperses.

The well was very popular, for the water level was near the surface and was termed a 'dipping well'. Moreover, it never failed. Some of our wells tended to dry up in periods of drought, but obviously, the Vicar's divine blessing brought rewards from a higher authority. It came to a sad ending however for, in the latter years of the 19th century, it was decided to close the well, after a dead baby's body had been discovered there. All the grounds, to the south, and east of the well, belonged to The Shrubbery, which I have written about elsewhere.

If we imagine the Green as the central hub, we now come to the last spoke in the wheel, before closing this chapter. I refer to Middle Lane known to the locals, for many years, as Waterses Lane. It was 30 years after the building of the railway and the local station, that the name of Station Road was officially adopted.

The Queens Head, in Station Road, is a very old village inn of humble origin. It started life as a cottage, became an ale house on the granting of a licence, and developed from there. Slight alterations were carried out, a signboard erected, suitably named, and the Queens Head was born!

Legend has it that Dick Turpin used to hide out at the Queens Head, whilst his scouts looked out for potential victims using the main road through Edmonton and Tottenham. We are discussing the early 1700's, when Green Lanes was little more than a drover's track. The legendary tales of Dick Turpin, and there are many, are difficult to prove or disprove. In a way, I suppose, that gives added appeal.

It is a fact that Turpin was the son of an Essex innkeeper, and that he did operate in the outlying districts to the north of London.

Sir William Paulin, with his wife Fanny (nee Mann) and their two daughters, Ina and Irene.

Rose Cottage, once the home of Thomas Hood.

The modern Queens Head bears no resemblance to the old ale house
that Dick Turpin might have known.

Moreover, he did have family ties in the locality, for his grandfather, Mr. Nott, was licensee of the Rose & Crown in Clay Hill, Enfield. Turpin was suspected of the murder of a gamekeeper in Epping Forest and, whilst evading the attentions of the Bow Street Runners, he is said to have gone into hiding at Camlet Moat in Trent Park. His connections, therefore, with the Queens Head in Winchmore Hill remain a distinct possibility, even though the evidence is slight and cannot be proven.

To the left of the inn was a small grocer's shop, with a cottage next door. There is a most revealing photograph taken in 1915, looking up the hill. The north side of the road is lined with trees, right up to the station. On the south side, the inn, cottage and shop project well into Station Road causing a narrow restriction of the highway at this point. It mattered little. People walk unhampered in the road and the only sign of traffic is one stationary bicycle. The shop was run by Mr. and Mrs. James Waters and the cottage was the family home, where James junior was born in 1844. His parents made a big impression on the village. They were such a kind and charismatic couple, that the road became known as Waterses Lane.

James junior and his wife continued in the family tradition as the much loved village grocers. They seldom left the district. Apart from work, James' main hobbies were his beloved cricket and running. He played several times with the Walker brothers and was one of Winchmore Hill's best players. As a runner, he competed against several other local athletes including the much acclaimed William (Rat) Hemington. The races were taken very seriously and the villagers would turn out and lay side bets on the result.

James Waters would certainly have some stories to tell, for he lived through a time of dramatic change. Just imagine, he was born 27 years before the railway arrived and 37 years before Southgate's separation from Edmonton. Yet, when he died at the age of 95, the Second World War had already begun. What a transformation he saw in his lifetime!

Mr. and Mrs. Waters left the old shop and their cottage and moved across the road next to Skinners premises (demolished in 1963). They continued their grocery business into the thirties. The brewers took over the old premises and the Queens Head was entirely rebuilt, to become a modern and much enlarged public house, which bears no relation to the old ale house that Dick Turpin might have known.

I should like to elaborate on William (Rat) Hemington, for he was an interesting character who lived in one of the Salisbury Cottages in Hoppers Road, where he brought up a family of 11 children.

At one of my lectures I made contact with Gwen Webb. William Hemington was her great-uncle, and, at time of writing, I understand that five of his children still survive. She confirmed the origin of his nickname, for he was in the habit of sucking out the raw eggs from their shells and returning them to their nest.

She also knew of William's training run which started at the entrance to the woods (now Broad Walk). Here he would hang his watch on a tree, then run along the footpath into Dog & Duck Lane (now Bourne Hill). From here he would run down the hill and return along Hoppers Road back to his starting point, where he would check his time. I measured the distance as just under 2 miles. I gather from other sources that this was also the course for competitive races, when the villagers could bet on their favourites. I am most grateful to Gwen Webb for passing on these stories and others about the Hemingtons.

I could go on and on. There are so many stories and people to write about. For all my omissions, I humbly apologise. I hope I have included some of the important and interesting stories that reflect a true image of our village as it was, and as it has now become. Our lives today are so different from the past. It is as well that we record the fact and reflect on days gone by.

# CHAPTER 5

## THE CRESSWELLS AND THE COMING OF THE RAILWAY

IN THE OLD village communities, there was inevitably a great dependence on certain key characters, whose help and co-operation would go a long way to ensure a happy and harmonious environment. The church itself, and all it stood for, was often the centrepiece but the great landowners with all their wealth and power, the farmers, the innkeepers, the blacksmiths, the wheelwrights, the tradesmen in general – they all had a large part to play.

High on the list was the village doctor, not just for his professional expertise, but for his role as a friend and comforter in times of need. I have already written about Doctor Fairweather in my book on Palmers Green.* His admirable service as a doctor and friend in that area had spanned some 54 years, whilst doctor John Cresswell was to serve Winchmore Hill for just half a century. They were both men of great ability, blended with kindness and patience, yet there the similarities end, for their circumstances differed widely.

Doctor Fairweather had to adapt to dramatic and rapid change. In 1882, when he commenced his practice, he would ride on horseback across the open countryside to visit his patients. How conditions, and the population, had changed by 1936 when he retired, then in his 81st year.

I know I have commented on this before but, in studying social history, one is struck by the fairly gradual changes in our environment through the centuries until one reaches the crossroads, when the nineteenth century drew to a close and the twentieth century began. Since then, two world wars have cast their shadows over the lives of millions. In many different spheres, it has been an era of unprecedented advancement, even within our own lifetimes. Never have the changes been so profound, neither have they been compressed before into so short a span.

This, however, was not the case with Doctor John Cresswell, for his practice of 50 years standing in Winchmore Hill drew to a close with his death in 1892, just 10 years after Doctor Fairweather had

*Mention of Doctor Fairweather reminds me that, since my book on Palmers Green was published (1988), there have been progressive and extensive alterations carried out to the properties in Aldermans Hill, particularly to those fine old houses at its western end that overlook Broomfield Park. Some have been 'converted' and others have been demolished in recent times. Doctor Fairweather's fine old house on the corner of Lakeside Road has gone, to be replaced by a complex of sheltered flats for the elderly. The doctor's house was one of the first houses to be built in Aldermans Hill, in 1905, following the sale of the Taylor estates.

established his. Notwithstanding the coming of the railway in 1871, which caused some immediate personal problems and disturbance (the demolition of his house and the enforced move into Grove Lodge), the changes Cresswell witnessed, by comparison and generally speaking, had much less impact on the locality and its people. The villagers' way of life in the 1870's and 1880's was soon to be transformed as the first half of this century materialised.

Let us, then, examine in more detail the life of Doctor John Cresswell and his influence on the village.

Richard Henry Cresswell (1782-1818) lived with his wife Henrietta (1790-1870) in some rooms just off St. Paul's Churchyard, and it was here that John Cresswell and his brothers were born. Richard died aged 36, just a week before his son John was born, and Henrietta, his wife, was to remain a widow for 52 years.

John Cresswell received his medical training at St. Bartholomew's Hospital, and his practical experience started when he was apprenticed to a Maidstone surgeon. Later on, he became attached to a practice in Derbyshire.

His association with Winchmore Hill began in 1842, when he was 24. It would appear that his predecessor, Doctor Radford, had not proved entirely satisfactory with the parish authorities (Edmonton), for he had been given six months notice to terminate his appointments. Doctor Cresswell purchased the practice and thus began a fifty year association with Winchmore Hill, during which time he and his family became an integral, I should say vital, part of village life.

The doctor came to live at No. 1 Trois Vase House in Hoppers Road and immediately made a great impression on his patients. As the years went by, he became one of the village's most loved stalwarts, for he was a character with many idiosyncrasies and unique qualities.

On 28th June 1852, he married his cousin, Frances Willink. The Willink family was of Dutch origins. They were married at St. James' Church, Pentonville. The church had no bell and Miss Willink chose Coronation Day* to get wed, so that every church bell in London should ring out to celebrate this momentous day in her life. The happy pair made the journey to Winchmore Hill in a poste-chaise drawn by a pair of white horses, one of which was ridden by the postillion. They dispensed with a honeymoon and settled at No. 1 Trois Vase House to start their married life.

*The 14th anniversary of the Coronation of Queen Victoria.

I should perhaps explain the exact position of Trois Vase House, which consisted of a pair of villas (Nos. 1 and 2). They were situated just on the eastern side of Hoppers Road, where the skew road bridge now spans the railway, nearly opposite Downes Court. The stables of each villa had originally been decorated with three stone vases, hence the name, though those on No. 1 were subsequently removed. The Independent Chapel (built in 1844) was next to the villas, just to the north. Except for a few small cottages and stable buildings facing Hoppers Road at this time, open fields surrounded the family home. Nearly opposite was the house lived in by Eaton, the carrier. His horses were particularly fine specimens and, when not pulling the carriages, they were allowed to recover in the lush meadows nearby.

The Cresswells had 2 children, Frank, who also became a doctor and Henrietta, who was to play such an important role in village life as she grew up in this very beautiful area, with such a happy family background. Henrietta was born on 15th February 1855 and it was shortly after her birth that her maternal grandmother, Mrs. Willink, came to live next door at No. 2.

The doctor's mother had already moved into a cottage in Vicars Moor Lane. At this time, before the railway arrived, there stood on the northern side of the lane a row of three charming cottages. They were quite a respectable size and stood well back from the lane, with colourful gardens bordered by low brick walls and picket fences. Mrs Cresswell lived in the cottage at the eastern end which had a wooden stable and hayloft attached, and at the side was a large garden, part of which is now the site of 'Inver', the first house on the eastern side of the railway. The old yew tree in the back garden of 'Inver' can still be seen today. This originally stood in the garden alongside Mrs. Willink's cottage.

These cottages in Vicars Moor Lane, like Trois Vase House and the Independent Chapel in Hoppers Road, were demolished to make way for the railway cutting and the laying of the tracks during 1870. Vicars Moor Lane was closed whilst the work on the railway bridge was in progress. The Great Northern Railway had acquired the necessary land and properties on which the lines would run.

On 1st January 1870, the doctor and his family, Mrs. Willink and the Church authorities were requested to vacate their premises and the demolition work began. The railway authorities had already acquired Grove Lodge, a large house at the top of Middle Lane (now Station Road), just above the railway station of today. This was let to Doctor Cresswell and the move was made. Young Henrietta was nearly 15 years old at the time. The doctor's mother was uprooted from her lovely cottage in Vicars Moor Lane to move in with her son at Grove Lodge. The upheaval proved too much for her and she died nearly three months later, on 19th March 1870, aged 81 years.

Grove Lodge was originally built by a Mr. Morgan, a wealthy papermaker, for his son Charles, who lived there for several years after his marriage. Mr. Morgan senior was then living in a house, the site of which is now the railway cutting between Vicars Moor Lane and Station Road. He was a noted greyhound owner with a pack of 30 to 40, which occasionally caused consternation in the village when they were allowed to exercise unmuzzled in the fields and lanes around the locality. He moved to Hazelwood House in Palmers Green.

As work on the railway progressed, the cutting for Winchmore Hill Station proved to be so near to Grove Lodge that the shrubs in the garden kept slipping over the edge, and had to be replanted. A retaining wall was built between the garden and the cutting, but the bricks were laid in freezing weather and the wall soon collapsed. It was later rebuilt.

Young Henrietta was at a most impressionable age and she describes the coming of the railway with much charm in her book 'Memories of a Lost Village'. The Ganger was called Dandy, a big north-countryman adorned with many large pearl buttons and a heavy silver watch chain. He ruled his men with a rod of iron and the hard working navvies, recruited mainly from Yorkshire and Lincolnshire, dared not fail him. Woe betide should any step out of line.

They would bring their food and tea cans to be heated on the great kitchen range at Grove Lodge, when they would curb their somewhat 'choice' language. Rough diamonds they may have been, and a long way from home, but they would respond with politeness and respect when it was accorded them. On Sundays and holidays, they discarded their working clothes and appeared resplendent in brightly coloured waistcoats and knee breeches.

Doctor John Cresswell was to continue in service as the village doctor for a total of 50 years, until his death at Grove Lodge on 9th November 1892, aged 74. His compass far exceeded the duties of a general practitioner. A fair and wise counsel, his advice was sought on a wide variety of issues. A kind and considerate man, he endeared himself to the village and his work as an artist was highly regarded. His skill as a doctor was unquestioned. For 50 years he brought every new inhabitant of Winchmore Hill into the world and saw most of the old inhabitants out. In between, he looked after and treated their ailments and became a friend to most.

The doctor always carried his sketch book with him and was a prolific water colour artist, recording the local scenes in much detail. His paintings are so valuable to us today recording as they do, the period in which he lived. He could appear very smart in his frock coat and silk hat but he did not always look the part. Never too fussy about his own appearance or style of dress, he would visit his patients on a large old-fashioned tricycle, with his trousers turned up so as not to catch in the pedals. As a young man, he was a crack shot who had won prizes at the National Rifles Association competitions held at Wimbledon.

Doctor John Cresswell loved his home and his adopted village, and slept away from home on only two or three occasions during his first 40 years in the practice. His wife Frances died in December 1886, aged 67, and there is a tablet in St. Paul's Church in her honour. Their home, Grove Lodge, will be remembered by many of my readers, for its connection with doctors and medicine was to continue right through to modern times. It was demolished in the 1960's to make way for Moor Park House (2a Wilson Street), the complex of flats which stands there today.

A few years after John Cresswell's death, his son, Doctor Frank Cresswell, moved into 'Cotterstock' at 42 Station Road. During my researches in 1989, a visit to the unsuspecting current occupiers of the house proved fruitful. There, above a window opening at ground floor level at the rear, I was shown a cast iron plate with the letters '18 F.C. 95' inscribed. The doctor must have incorporated this in the building nearly a century ago. Doctor Frank Cresswell, an accomplished amateur photographer, was forced to give up medicine because of failing eyesight. He moved to Leicestershire in 1902-3 and died a few years later.

Henrietta, 37 years old at the time of her father's death, moved into 16 Station Road which she named 'Cheslyn', after some of her ancestors, the Cheslyns of Leicestershire. She also left the district at the turn of the century to settle in Dumfries. From there she moved to Cumbria where she eventually purchased 'Lambgill', set in a lovely position in Watermillock overlooking Ullswater, where she died on 20th October 1931.

Some years ago I visited the church and its graveyard in Watermillock where Henrietta's body lies next to that of her cousin 'Stasia' (Miss C.M. Anastasia Cresswell), who lived with her and predeceased her by two or three years. I visited the charming cottage she had lived in, with glorious views over the lake, and was made most welcome by the current owners who were interested in all I could tell them about Miss Cresswell and her connections with Winchmore Hill.

Henrietta Cresswell (1855-1931) was a very talented lady. She was a fine water colour artist and had several flower studies accepted and exhibited at the Royal Academy. She was a gifted writer, both in poetry and prose, a skilled and artistic needlewoman, botanist, horticulturist and naturalist, an ardent lover of wild flowers, wild birds and the wild life of countryside and shore throughout Britain. She was a good photographer, a fine horsewoman and an expert on the breeds of poultry, cats and dogs. Apart from her artistic talents, she was also a very practical handyman, making her own poultry houses, kennels, kitchen cabinets and bookshelves etc. A very busy and vital lady indeed.

She has left with us the legacy of her delightful book and, more particularly, the paintings and sketches of her father, which she was kind enough to donate to the authorities when she left the district at the turn of the century.

She loved her family home and her family life. It shines through on every page, when she speaks of her parents, her brother and her two grandmothers. She was always called 'Winifred' by grandmother Cresswell who lived in Vicars Moor Lane and Henrietta writes with obvious joy of the days she would play in the garden there, with her brother, Frank. One of her poems, written in 1913, makes reference to these happy times and I quote some of her verses:—


## MY GRANDMOTHER'S GARDEN

Sweet lavender, how it recalls
A garden that I erstwhile knew,
A weeping ash, a holly hedge,
Some winding paths, a mighty yew.

The garden where we used to play,
Where flowers bloomed the whole year round,
A haven on a summer's day,
Where rest and peace were ever found.

Sweet rosemary and lavender,
Carnations, pinks and picotees,
What luscious fragrance filled the air!
Beneath the laden apple trees.

The vision fades, for all are gone,
The little house, two centuries old!
The dear in-dwellers of the home
For whom my love can ne'er wax cold.

But still above the iron road,
Where crowded trains go rushing by,
And close beside a busy street
There stands erect the ancient yew.

The iron road referred to is the railway, and the ancient yew is the one I have already referred to, still visible in the back garden of 'Inver'.

Henrietta often accompanied her father on his daily round. It was a different world then and life was lived at a much more leisurely pace. Henrietta was but 4 years old when she stood with her father in the nursery garden (the present day site of Truro House) in Palmers Green, to witness the sighting of the Great Comet in 1858. It made such a great impression on her that, years later, she could still recall and record the scene in great detail and with much charm.

In 1862, when Henrietta was seven years old, her father took her to the 'Cart on the Green', a large horse-drawn gypsy type caravan which pitched on the Green near the Kings Head corner, extolling the magic of photography. It was a new attraction in the village and caused great excitement.

One entered by mounting some steps through a doorway into a carpeted 'studio'. There was a window, fringed with lace curtains, and a small table and chair as the necessary props. After much to-ing and fro-ing, the sitter was asked to 'freeze' for at least half a minute, and the photographer would then retire to the other room, a windowless sanctum where the mysterious process was completed.

Our local history department still has those original photographs of the doctor (then 44 years old) and Henrietta (7), taken in 1862. Even with their comparatively crude equipment and techniques, the photographs tell us a great deal of the skill and expertise of those early pioneers of photography.

In 'Memories of a Lost Village', the chapter that gave me the most pleasure was the one entitled 'The Wood', which Henrietta describes as a magical place where she played as a child. Her memory remained undimmed with the passing of time and she captures the wonderment and thrill of secret hiding places, amidst the beauty of the forest, with all the wide-eyed innocence of youth.

In her days the footpath still ran from Dog & Duck Lane (Bourne Hill), through the woods, to the hamlet of Winchmore Hill on the line of, what is now, Broad Walk. We entered through a stile and were immediately in dense woodland. We were walking through Mr. Taylor's estates. There was a picket fence to our left and beyond, the vast expanse of Grovelands. Soon we passed the Keeper's Cottage. On the right and to the east, the wild unspoilt woodland stretched away to Hoppers Road. Miss Cresswell continues: —

It was an Enchanted Forest, millions of miles from London or even from the pond on the green; wild and remote and mysterious, bounded only by dinner time, tea time, or the short winter twilight. When in the heart of the wood, it was easy to realise that at one time there had been continuous forest land covering the greater part of Middlesex; and to feel that, perhaps, for a thousand years, this corner of England had remained unaltered.

Those who have heard the voices of the woods, and loved their whisperings in childhood, will hear them calling for ever in the after years, calling them to wild places, to country sights and sounds, to the unspoilt corners of the land, where they can forget that crowds, and cities, and struggling suburbs even exist. The Spirit of the Woods and the Spirit of the Hills know their own, and when they call, their own must go forth and do them homage.

Henrietta Cresswell became an easily recognisable figure in the village. In her childhood, she had always been perplexed by her hair. The fashion of the day was for a child to have a centre parting and an abundance of curls. Her mother tried hard to get Henrietta's hair to conform with a 'fixative' and the constant use of curlers during sleep.

As she grew up, Henrietta decided to let her hair (which she describes as nondescript) obey the laws of nature. She had it cut very short, i.e. shingled, and let the natural parting on the left side remain. This would not be considered exceptional today but, at the turn of the century, it was unusual to say the least and drew

A remarkable photograph of Doctor Cresswell, taken in 1862,
in the 'Cart on the Green.'

*(above left)*
Henrietta Cresswell, aged 7, in
the 'studio' on the Green in 1862,
when she was taken there by her
father, whose picture appears on
a previous page.

*(above right)*
Miss Cresswell was a lady of
many talents.

*(lower right)*
This photograph was taken by
Miss Cresswell of her father,
aged 71.

considerable attention to her so-called mannish appearance.

In her writings Henrietta recalls, with some humour, that she could not step out of a train on a railway platform without a chorus of 'Get yer 'air cut' from the loafers and that, on one occasion, the guard addressed her 'Beg pardon, sir, but this is a ladies carriage' until he realised his mistake. She persisted, however, with the 'new style', which she was happy with, and it soon became accepted.

Henrietta was a lady of such wide and diverse talents that there are many stories to tell. She left the village that she loved in her mid-forties. As the twentieth century began, so the changes became more marked and, the village that she once knew, gradually succumbed to the spread of London's surburbia. 'Memories of a Lost Village' was first published in 1907. The title bears out of her own feelings. Was the village already 'lost' by that time, and what would she think of Winchmore Hill today?

In my researches, I came across a poem that she wrote some 5 years before her death. Perhaps it sums up, best of all, her attitude to life:-

### THE OTHER SIDE

Effort is never lost, effort for right,
The man who tried his best with all his might
Gains in himself, yet more of strength and power,
By overcoming self, from hour to hour.
We must go up or down, we cannot rest,
Sink to decay, or climb to reach the best;
And though each summit shows us hills above,
Our patience and our faithfulness to prove;
We know full well, some hill will be the last,
And rest must come when that is safely past.
Some day we shall across the sombre tide
With joy behold that glorious Other Side.
God grant that, held aloft by faith and prayer,
Our souls at last may land in safety there.

And so the Cresswell connections with Winchmore Hill were severed. Their contributions towards village life had been sustained and invaluable. The community had been enriched by their presence, and was the poorer for their passing.

This is perhaps an appropriate place to enlarge on some other aspects of the coming of the railway. In spite of Mr. Taylor's opposition, rumours had abounded for many years that there was to be an extended branch line of the Great Northern Railway built from Wood Green, through Palmers Green and Winchmore Hill, out to Enfield, a distance of just over 4 miles.

Enfield Town had already been put on the railway map in 1849, with the construction of a branch line from Angel Road (Water Lane), with an intermediate station at Lower Edmonton. The Eastern Counties Railway, who initiated the scheme, later joined forces with other East Anglian railways to form a new company, the Great Eastern Railway, in 1862. All this had virtually no effect on Palmers Green or Winchmore Hill, which remained as quiet and sleepy backwaters. In 1872, a direct line, from Liverpool Street to Enfield, was opened and the station in Southbury Road was completely rebuilt.

Meanwhile, the village of Winchmore Hill was awoken from its slumbers in the summer of 1869, when the gangs arrived with their picks, shovels and barrows. They set to work with great gusto, initially in the open fields north of Vicars Moor Lane. Within a few days, rows of wooden huts appeared and Firbank's navvies made themselves comfortable in their temporary homes. Work had already started at the Enfield (Windmill Hill) and Wood Green ends.

The new line was originally scheduled to open in 1870. This date can be seen at both Palmers Green and Winchmore Hill stations, where it has been cast on the girders supporting the bridge and station buildings immediately above the track, in both cases. There were, however, unforeseen problems encountered in the construction, which led to delays.

In the Winchmore Hill N21 area there are four road bridges – Hoppers Road, Compton Road, Middle Lane (which became Station Road in 1902) and Vicars Moor Lane, also two railway bridges over Green Dragon Lane and Vera Avenue.

In addition, John Donnithorne Taylor insisted on the construction of a private bridge (since demolished) over the line, to give his farmcarts access to Hoppers Road. This was some 220 yards to the south of the skew bridge in that road. 'JDT' was bitterly opposed to the railway's expansion into the area and did all he could to stop it. As the greatest landowner in our midst, his policy had been consistently one of conservation. He realised that improved communication would only serve to increase the pressure from the developers, something he had fought to withstand all his life.

He continued to fight. He is thought to have been behind a horse bus service to the City, which ran in competition with the railway until 1879. As a further gesture of his disapproval, he refused to travel on the new line and preferred to journey to Colney Hatch Station (now called New Southgate), whence he caught the train into town.

The main construction problem locally, however, was the extensive embankment needed to span the wide valley to the north of the village. The clay embankments had a tendency to 'slip', causing undulations in the track. The level of Green Dragon Lane, known to the villagers as Dog Kennel Lane, was raised and the stream culverted under the new road surface. Thus a familiar 'watersplash' and footbridge disappeared from the scene.

There were other local 'difficulties'. Miss Cresswell recounts that a certain mischievous gentleman (we are not told his name) caused havoc by moving all the marking pegs in his garden to different, quite arbitrary, positions without the contractors knowledge. It caused quite serious delay. Although the incident is not without humour, it is doubtful if the contractors shared the joke at the time.

At last the opening date for the railway was announced – 1st April 1871. Could it really be true or was someone playing an April Fools prank? On the night of 31st March 1871, all was ready. The station was at last completed and the final coat of paint had been applied. A fusilade of bangs shook the village, as the navvies let off a farewell celebration. Their long arduous task, in which five of their colleagues had tragically lost their lives, was finally over. The next morning, three new stations (Palmers Green, Winchmore Hill and Enfield) were open for business, with 16 Up and 15 Down trains a day on weekdays and five each way on Sundays.

The immediate effect on Winchmore Hill was far from dramatic. The village carried on in its quiet, unhurried way but the prophets, no doubt, could see the omens and recognise the signs. The wall had been breached and the trickle, given time, would gather pace as the new twentieth century was born.

I continually find myself referring to the old Ordnance Survey maps of the district, as they contribute so much to our interpretation of the scene. One must study them long and hard, and gradually the picture takes shape. The beauty and peace of the countryside was here on our doorsteps, less than a century ago. No wonder Doctor Cresswell always had his sketch book handy, and no wonder his patients were sometimes kept waiting, when he became distracted from his professional calling.

His sketch looking north from Green Dragon Lane is a case in point. We see a gateway, where Old Park Ridings joins today and beyond, a green valley backed by the hills in the distance, on the other side of Salmons Brook.

The 2nd edition of Ordnance Survey (1897) paints its own picture of the scene the doctor wished to convey. There was Filcap's Farm on the north side of Green Dragon Lane, where Landra Gardens enters today, Old Park Farm away to the north in Enfield territory, the mansion of Old Park set in beautiful surroundings and nearby Pike's Farm (Old Park Grange). All around is open countryside, farmland and orchards. The spire of St. Mary Magdalene at the top of Windmill Hill oversees all with its lordly presence.

The old map shows the scene as it was, 26 years after the arrival of the railway. We can see the line clearly marked, terminating at Enfield Station near the foot of Windmill Hill. The whole area north of Green Dragon Lane is a vista of open countryside, bounded by Chase Road in the west, the Green Lanes and Bush Hill in the east, and East Barnet Road (Bramley Road and Enfield Road) to the north. It represents a huge panorama, unspoilt by development. Only a very rural and unfinished World's End Lane divides the area.

A hundred years ago, the top of Green Dragon Lane was known as Park Corner. Worlds End Lane was half a mile long and simply led to a hollow by the side of a small stream that fed into Salmons Brook. We can trace that same spot today. Then, Worlds End seemed an apt name for such a place, untouched by man. Beyond, and all around, was an endless view of nature's beauty, in a setting of peace and serenity. Nearly all the land to the east of this lane was once part of the Old Park estate, the history of which I have covered in Chapter 7.

In 1906, major construction work was resumed in extending the railway northwards from Enfield, this being all part of the originally conceived Hertford Loop. A new line had to be constructed from a point south of the Enfield terminus, the new track then diverging slightly to the east of the old, to meet up with a new bridge crossing Windmill Hill. The new alignment was necessary to give the bridge sufficient headroom above the roadway, thus avoiding the necessity of a level crossing. In Windmill Hill, a new station was built slightly downhill from the old.

In 1923, this was renamed Enfield Chase Station, to distinguish it from the Town Station which stood in Southbury Road. By 1910, the new line had reached Cuffley.

As these works progressed, development was also going ahead on

A nostalgic look down Station Road, showing the carriages awaiting the arrival of their masters' train.

The station in 1989. Can you spot the differences?

the existing part of the line, south of Enfield Station, on those same open fields we have just explored. It was known as the Grange Estate, having taken its name from the nearby Old Park Grange, sadly razed to the ground with the construction of the Cuffley extension, when the re-alignment of the track became necessary.

The estate was laid out by Mr. Richard Metherell & Son of Winchmore Hill, who invited the Great Northern Railway authorities to build a new station, to serve a new community. It was obviously going to enhance the value of his properties considerably, if there was to be easy rail access. In seeking their agreement, he offered to give up several acres of land to accommodate the new station and its approaches, and undertook to build a stated number of houses, within a specified time. The railway authorities could foresee the potential in the growth of a new area, which would bring them many new fare-paying customers.

Although completion of Grange Park Station was originally planned for 1908, it finally came into being on 4th April 1910, simultaneously with the opening of the Cuffley extension.

The development also saw the end of Old Park Grange. This centuries-old building had originally served as a hunting lodge and it stood roughly where 83 Old Park Ridings exists today, just south of the junction with The Chine, near the top of the hill. Additions had been made through the years to transform it into a farmhouse, latterly known as Pike's farm. The last resident farmer to occupy the old house was Franklin Pike, who vacated the tenancy of the farm and orchards in 1904. Mr. and Mrs. Pike were well known in the village and might be seen with their 6 children in a commodious wagonette, drawn by a sturdy white horse, driving to the Congregational Church in Compton Road every Sunday morning, with unfailing regularity.

On its north side, Old Park Grange adjoined the grounds of Chase Park. This large house fell similarly to the demands of the rail extension to Cuffley. Its position was just to the east of today's railway, towards the northern end of Old Park Avenue. On the southern side of Old Park Grange was Enfield Old Park, then owned by Mr. J.W. Ford, whose mansion is now used as the golf clubhouse. Carr's Lane was the carriage approach from Bush Hill to Chase Park, which was once owned by the Carr family. The advent of the railway extension towards Hertford brought about a re-siting of part of the railroad, and cost dearly. It caused the demolition of both Chase Park and Old Park Grange.

Richard Metherell, who lived at Elmscott in Bush Hill, purchased the Grange estate from Lord Currie, and his farm bailiff occupied the house for a time. The extent of the old farm had long been known as Pike's Fields, after the family who last worked it. It was an area of great beauty, lying as it did in the valley of Salmons Brook, with gentle hills on either side. There were well-used footpaths through the fields and orchards, providing lovely walks for the villagers from Green Dragon Lane across to Enfield.

At one time, Charles Lamb and his sister Mary were known to be regular users of these footpaths. They lived in Gentlemans Row and Chase Side, Enfield, during the period 1825 to 1833. They were friends of Thomas Hood, who lived at Rose Cottage in Vicars Moor Lane and they were also valued customers of Udalls, the high class draper's shop on Winchmore Hill Green. Their visits would have taken them across the fields and back on many occasions.

Mr. Metherell began by straightening and widening the lower end of Green Dragon Lane, and building on the northern side of the lane, between Bush Hill and Old Park Ridings. Next, in conjunction with his son, he laid out and constructed the roads Old Park Ridings, The Chine and the Grangeway, including the building of two road bridges over Salmons Brook.

With the new station operating from 1910, the development continued at a good rate, until interrupted by the outbreak of war in 1914. There are many letters and editorials in the columns of our local newspapers of the time, deeply regretting the disappearance of this once completely rural scene. There are also articles, particularly in 'The Recorder', lavishing praise on Mr. Metherell for the quality of his workmanship and for his good taste and care in the setting out of the estate. They read like advertisement features, but are obviously meant to reflect independent comment and opinion.

The scene was changing, but it was a gradual process. For many years the undeveloped portions of the fields and orchards were farmed by Messrs. A. Stapleton & Sons, well known dairymen of the time.

In 1916, Richard Metherell purchased the Thorney Manor estate, Thorney Island, West Sussex, and moved in, together with his son. They farmed there, on a very large scale for about 14 years.

Their industry and enterprise in developing Grange Park and the surrounding areas in the early part of this century was a major contribution. The legacy of their work endures today. Grange Park remains one of the more desirable areas in which to live. The properties are well built and, in spite of the spread of suburbia, Grange Park has struggled (and to an extent succeeded) in retaining its own identity.

It is worthwhile to explore Grange Park Station. The station itself is at street level, with long ramped walkways leading us up to the platform levels. One can appreciate the huge undertaking required to build these embankments, to carry the track across the valley. On a clear day we get some superb views of the locality from the station platforms. We can look around in all directions and pick out the various landmarks.

I found myself thinking of the old doctor, sketch book at the ready, and wondered how much he would have recognised from the old days. No longer would he visit his patients on horseback or, indeed, his quaint old tricycle. We can no longer walk over Pike's Fields or linger in the orchard by Salmons Brook, in the heat of a lazy summer's afternoon. That is all in the past. We have to accept the present, learn from our mistakes and try to steer to a better future. We owe that to the generations to come.

# CHAPTER 6

## BY THE GREEN LANES

THE MAIN ARTERY in the area is Green Lanes and I thought it might be worthwhile for us to travel along the route. Let us start on the extreme southern border, near Barrowell Green, and head northwards.

Originally no more than a drover's track, they really were green lanes even up to the turn of the century. For much of the way, mature trees lined the road forming a canopy of green above. The road frontages were little developed and beyond, as far as the eye could see, was the open countryside.

In my books, the basis I have used for the division of Southgate, Palmers Green and Winchmore Hill has been the postal districts of N14, N13 and N21 respectively. It is a far from perfect method, yet better than any other I could devise. Occasionally, near the boundaries, it has created problems.

Sometimes I have erred deliberately, as in the case of Palmers Green High School. The school is now in N21 but it started life as Miss Hum's at No. 1 Osborne Road N13 and, by its very name, would still seem to belong to Palmers Green. My omission of Winchmore Hill Methodist Church from my Palmers Green book was a complete oversight on my part for the church is clearly within the N13 district. Once again, however, the name would suggest otherwise, so I hope you will excuse its inclusion here in N21.

Thomas Kelsey, a builder and Congregationalist, moved from Stamford Hill to Winchmore Hill in the 1850's. He built extensively in the Bowes Park area and on the Eaton Park estate, and made his home at Highfield House, to which I have referred later in the chapter. In 1879, he offered a plot of land to the Finsbury Park Wesleyan Methodist Circuit, on condition that they built a chapel on the site and arranged regular services. Winchmore Hill was still a quiet country village and there were doubts expressed as to whether they could muster enough support. A simple, small chapel of much appeal was built in 1880 and opened for worship the following year. The site was opposite Barrowell Green, set well back from the Green Lanes in a very rural setting.

After a few successful years, the congregation dwindled. In 1884, the first Trust was formed at a meeting in the Wood Green chapel. Mr. Kelsey died the following year. In 1886, Mr. A.H. Mummery was asked to help revive the Society which was at a very low ebb. A turning point came with the appointment of Rev. A.E. Witham in 1905, with the pastoral care of Bowes Park and Winchmore Hill within his jurisdiction. The partition, which separated the Sunday School from the Chapel, had to be removed to allow a maximum of 186 seats. In 1906, land frontage to a depth of 10 feet was lost, this being required by the authorities for road widening to accommodate the trams, which were to arrive the following year. The £100 compensation was used to purchase a second-hand organ.

During the years 1906-8, extensive housebuilding took place in Woodberry Avenue, Fernleigh Road, Hoppers Road and other roads nearby and it was obvious that a much larger house of worship would soon be needed. Resources were being stretched at the time, as a new Methodist Church was also being built in Bowes Park, for which all available funds were needed.

In 1909, Rev. William Middleton was appointed as minister in charge of Winchmore Hill. Certain members of the Trust thought that the new church should be built on a vacant site in Bourne Hill near the Pound but, at a crucial meeting in 1910, it was decided by 31 votes to 4 that the church should be built on the Green Lanes site, on the land in front of the existing chapel. The work went ahead and a fine new church was opened for worship on 28th September 1912.

The Methodists were gaining strength in the area with a strong following at The Bourne. Following the opening of the railway station at Grange Park and the subsequent development there, a new society was formed. In 1921 a house in Fernleigh Road was purchased as the Manse which, in 1948, was transferred to a house in Hoodcote Gardens.

Since the Second World War, a changing population has led to a diminished congregation and, in recent years, we have seen the building works completed in effectively reducing the size of the church. The traditional and rather ornate front of the church has been demolished and rebuilt in a much plainer style, set well back from the highway. A car park has been formed in the space provided.

All through the years the Church has continued to adapt to the fluctuating needs of its members and, in the words of Mr. R.F. Farrant, a stalwart of the Church:- 'The history is a record of committed, devoted and determined people, inspired by the Holy Spirit, who built and maintained a church that they, and those who follow them, should have a place in which to worship and serve their God.'

Winchmore Hill Methodist Church, built in 1912, has developed from the original chapel built in 1880. The lower picture shows the result of recent rebuilding.

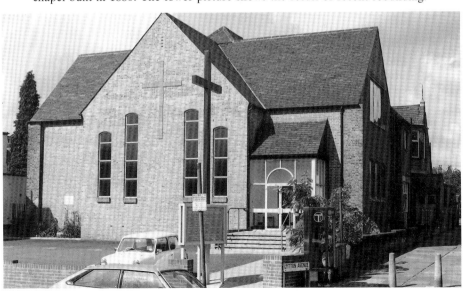

Holy Trinity was built in 1908 to serve a growing population on the eastern side of the parish.

Those words are no less sincere and no less true because they are shared with many others of pioneer spirit who helped to establish the churches in our midst, nearly 100 years ago.

By the church, next to Lytton Avenue, are a couple of shops where Miller & Hard, the newsagents and tobacconists, once operated. Many of us will recall Mr. Miller and his assistant Miss Jay, who served us with such pleasantness and good humour during the war years. As we travel north past Barrowell Green, we can see on our right, running parallel to the road, the waters of the New River flowing quietly towards London. More of that anon.

On our left, reference to the 1867 O.S. Map shows the whole area to the west of the Green Lanes, bounded by Hoppers Road in the west and Back Lane (Compton Road) in the north, as open and undeveloped. This was known as Highfield Park with its mansion, Highfield House, which could be entered off Hoppers Road past a lodge and down a very attractive driveway. By the beginning of the First World War, the area was all built upon, with the exception of a once fine sports ground known to me originally as Bart's (St. Bartholomew's Sports Ground). The ground opened in June 1895 with Dr. Frank Cresswell a prime mover in securing it for the hospital. During the Second World War, it was used by the Stationers' Company's School under the jurisdiction of our County Council. I have played both soccer and cricket there. In its prime, it was a superb ground up to county standard, always tended by an expert groundsman and his staff.

At the time of writing, it is under threat and may be swallowed up in a vast supermarket development. Behind the stock brick wall bordering the Green Lanes, there is a sorry sight to see now. The ground is uncared for and the hallowed turf, once mollycoddled to perfection, is waving in hay. The pavilion, which has seen such happy times, stands forlorn and neglected.* No longer does the shout 'Howzat!' echo round the ground, nor do the bowlers' arms climb skywards in exultation. The innings has come to a close.

Henrietta Cresswell mentions Highfield House and its park, where she played as a child, as she recounts the journey by horsebus from the Flower Pot in Bishopsgate Street to Winchmore Hill:-

Then the leafy vista of Hoppers Road came in view, with the first cottages of the Hill in the distance. It was a beautiful road.

---

*The pavilion has since been demolished.

On the left were pines and larches, beeches and oaks, old forest land and newer plantations, an unspoilt virgin woodland. There were trees that were centuries old, and even the fields were full of fine timber. The hedgerows were bowers of hawthorn, a perfect snowstorm of bloom in maytime. The Little Wonder* stopped at the gates of Highfield Park, where a fine avenue stretched away to the house. A peacock was strutting up and down, and circling round to display the glories of his expanded tail.

'Aunt' Bury, the gatekeeper, came out of the hexagonal thatched lodge for a parcel she had been expecting. The peacock was full of hope when he saw her, and a flock of white turkeys came forward hastily to know if it were feeding time. The heavy iron gates clanked to, and the horses strained at their collars to start afresh. A row of tall Lombardy populars was passed, and then the Doctor's house†, where the scent of the sweet-briar hedge mingled with the fragrance of climbing roses. Next door stood a white brick chapel.

Highfield House, Georgian in style, was built in the early 1800's. It had a lodge in Hoppers Road, to which Miss Cresswell refers in the extract quoted, and an imposing entrance drive, where Arundel Gardens exists today. The basement walls were double and it was possible for a small man or boy to walk around the house between the inner and outer walls. At one time Captain Arlow, a captain in the Life Guards and his wife, the daughter of a peer, lived here. Arlow Road later took his name.

Thomas Kelsey, who gave some land to the Methodists for the building of their chapel, was followed by Mr. Wilkinson who bought Highfield House and some of its park in 1895. A billiard room was added on the west side and a large 'Winter Garden', complete with dance floor, on the east side. It appears the family were fond of celebrations and large parties, which would be held in these very pleasant surroundings. At one time, the house was supposed to be haunted by a ghost with clanking chains. However, during some alterations to the fireplace, a long length of chain was discovered, suspended in the flue. This had originally supported the turnspit. The mystery was solved for, in high winds, this chain would clank against the side of the chimney.

Though the park had long been absorbed, the house, situated on the corner of Arundel Gardens and Haslemere Road, survived until

*Name of the omnibus.
†Refers to Trois Vase House and the old independent chapel next door to which I referred in greater detail in Chapters 3 and 5.

108

1952. It will be remembered by many as Winchmore Hill High School for Girls (Miss Chislett's), though its last years were spent as an Auxiliary Fire Station, during the 1939-45 War. It fell into disrepair and was purchased by the Council in 1952, when it was demolished to make way for new flats and housing. The pleasant development has retained some of the trees, in particular a magnificent Cedar of Lebanon on the lawns in front of the flats.

We go past Winchmore Hill Police Station, built in 1915. The place has that indefinable character sadly lacking in the modern stations I have seen. We half expect to bump into P.C. Dixon of Dock Green on our way in. If the supermarket should ever arrive, or whatever other development is planned, let us hope they do not pull the station down and rebuild in modern style. Regretfully, change for change's sake often seems to apply these days. Let us hold on to our station, supermarket or no supermarket.

Next door is what most of us remember as Brimley's timber yard. In the last decade it has been bought out by Sandell Perkins, timber and builders' merchants, who have completely reorganised the whole complex. At least the tradition remains, for we can still buy timber there for all our needs, even if we are expected to think in metric terms, instead of feet and inches. More's the pity.

Winchmore Hill Baptist Church, on the southern corner of Compton Road as it sweeps into Green Lanes, was opened in 1907. However, its roots go back to pre-1670 days, when the Glasshouse Yard Baptist Church was established in an alley off Goswell Road where it joins Aldersgate in the City. The present Winchmore Hill Church is a direct lineal descendant of this, one of the oldest Baptist churches in the country.

It was early this century when the secretary of the London Baptist Association, Reverend John Bradford, was prospecting for a new site for the church, which had by now moved to Bethnal Green Road. He decided on Winchmore Hill, where a well-known local builder Mr. Edmondson, himself a Baptist, gave the present site to John Bradford to build his new church. A small group of similar faith was already worshipping at the home of Mrs. Gosden in Station Road. They joined forces with 18 members from the Bethnal Green church and worshipped, for a time, in the Collegiate School, whilst the new edifice was being built. It was opened and dedicated in 1907, just 2 years after the Baptist Church in Palmers Green was born.

At Winchmore Hill the Sunday School, which began in 1910, was housed in the left hand, or south east, side of the main church. The attendance soon grew to 112, spilling over into the upper and lower schoolrooms. A normal weekday school operated here through the years under various guises but latterly, since the early 1920's, as St. Olave's High School for Girls & Boys with Miss A.B. Buckley, the Principal and Headmistress. My wife, sister and brother-in-law all attended here, at the school known locally as 'Miss Buck's'. The school continued through the wartime period with closure coming in the later 1940's.

In 1926 the Bethnal Green premises, which had been let to the Jewish community to be used as a synagogue, were sold, thus enabling the church's building debt to be cleared. At the same time, a fund was set up for the building of Carey Hall, which was opened in 1928. The Winchmore Hill Baptists were, by now, well established and they have continued to play their part in the religious and social life of the district.

'The Cedars,' on the corner with Highfield Road, is the site of one of the old houses of the district. Not a great deal is known about its origins, except that a house stood there in 1800, thought to be smaller than the one we know in modern times. In the latter part of the last century, a Mr. Perigrene Purvis owned and lived in the house, then stated to be a residence of considerable charm with grounds on both sides of the New River. When Mr. Purvis died around 1905, the property was sold and the land on the east side of the River was detached, allowing Cedars Road and the houses to be built.

The house gets its name from the two large cedar trees that grew in the front garden facing on to Green Lanes, one on either side of the entrance pathway. On the night of the great gale on 28th March 1916, one of the trees was completely blown down, thereby disturbing the roots of the other, which survived for a couple more years before it had to be removed.

Mr. Purvis was a bachelor and a collector of rare and beautiful objects, with which he filled his home, said to resemble a small museum. When Mr. Westoby, the estate agent, bought the premises, he is said to have sold the knobs and finger plates on some of the doors to a dealer. They were of old Chelsea china and believed to be quite valuable. Cedar House, as it is now called, is currently occupied by a firm of chartered accountants.

On the other corner of Highfield Road stands the garage. Between the garage and Holy Trinity stood The Chestnuts and

Highfield Grange, both backing on to the New River, on land now occupied by the Duncan Court flats. Highfield Grange was an old Georgian, 3 storey, red-brick house said to have started life as a workhouse, which then became a private lunatic asylum. It is said that Mary Lamb was brought here several times by brother Charles during her temporary periods of insanity, to undergo rest and treatment. This would have been between 1825 and 1834, when the Lambs were living in Enfield and latterly in Edmonton.

The house was later lived in by Mr. Houlder, a solicitor and Clerk of the Edmonton Local Board of Health, who created a beautiful garden at the rear. The Houlders left in 1892. In its latter years, the house became run down and, during the first decade of this century, was used as a laundry. Eventually the roof fell in and the premises were demolished.

The Holy Trinity Church, on the corner with Queens Avenue, suffered a terrible blow in 1978 when, during building operations, a major fire broke out. The damage was extensive and it says much for the spirit and resilience of its members that restoration has been made so rapidly and effectively.

The church had been built in 1908, largely due to the efforts of the Reverend A.J.B. Dewdney. He had become vicar of St. Paul's Church in Church Hill on 8th May 1901. He readily accepted that further houses of worship would soon be needed in outlying parts of the parish. St. Andrew's Church was built in Chase Side, Southgate in 1903 and a Mission Hall was opened in Winchmore Hill Road in 1905. On the eastern side of the parish, the Mission Hall in Highfield Road was proving inadequate for the growing population. A site for a new church to cost £8,000 had been offered by the Busk Trustees but Holy Trinity was eventually built on the present site in Green Lanes, which was given by Mr. Edmondson in 1907.

The Rev. A.J.B. Dewdney helped to organise fund raising activities with a target of £5,000, the sum needed to build the first part of the new church. There would be an initial seating capacity of 500, later to be increased to 750 when the chancel was added. The Reverend's efforts came to fruition with the dedication of the Church of the Holy Trinity by the Bishop of Islington on 14th June 1908. Sadly, by then, Mr. Dewdney had been compelled to resign the living of St. Paul's because of ill-health. However, before emigrating to Canada in 1909, he had the joy of preaching at the new church for which he had laboured, Holy Trinity.

The church was consecrated as a parish church in 1913 and the

Hall opened in 1921. 25 years after its birth, in October 1933, the consecration of the chancel and the dedication of the vestries was performed by the Lord Bishop of Willesden. The fire of 1978 was a serious blow, but it was another story of triumph over adversity when the Bishop of Edmonton dedicated the restored church on 20th February 1982. A few months later, at a Mass of thanksgiving for the completion of the restoration, the Lord Bishop of London came to dedicate the new parish hall and unveil a commemorative plaque.

We have arrived at the Broadway, now a bustling, busy centre for shopping. We must not look upon this as the heart of the old village, for that lies up the hill around the Green. Here, the development is comparatively modern.

I have a photograph taken in 1902, looking north, which shows this stretch of Green Lanes as quite narrow and lined with mature trees, their branches linking overhead. The setting is completely rural, with picket fences and open fields and farmland on either side. There are no pavements as we know them, just raised gravelled footpaths on either side. A lady in charge of a pram rests by the side of the roadway and a very early motor car approaches at pedestrian pace. In the distance, facing us, we can see a pair of houses in Station Road, numbers 4 and 6, which remain to this day.

The decision had been made to extend the tramway northwards from Manor House. Green Lanes was widened and the Broadway complex of shops was built in 1904-5, much encouraged by the coming of the trams in 1907, which made the area fully accessible. This applied to other areas along the route further north, around the Green Dragon and Masons Corner areas. The Green Lanes became green no longer, as the shops spread along the main road to serve a growing local community.

I have included a small Directory of the Broadway shops at the end of the book, with comparison over a 50 year period. i.e. as they traded in 1939 and as they are today in 1989. My Palmers Green Directory proved very popular as it brought back many memories to older residents. The Broadway remains a much smaller shopping centre of less renown, nevertheless I hope the comparison will be of interest.

With the family based in Farm Road, these shops provided for our everyday needs, not only throughout the last war but for some years before and since. I include some of my own recollections, concerning them, in Chapter 9, rather than quote them here in, what has already become, a long chapter. I hope you understand.

How the Broadway appeared in 1902, looking north.

The busy shops of today, looking south.

The Capitol cinema, remembered with much affection.

Capitol House is now occupied by the Inland Revenue.

We glance at the narrow hump-backed bridges, with their separate pedestrian access, leading to Fords Grove and Farm Road. The bridges are a real hazard today, as they are barely wide enough for two vehicles to pass. A public convenience has long featured on the triangle of land at the junction.

Just at the top of Farm Road, tight on the banks of the New River, are the buildings of the old Collegiate School. It was one of our more important private schools, of which there were many, and which formed a significant part of the overall education system at that time. The school was founded in 1906 by Mr. J. Temblett-Wood, headmaster, who lived in a house next to the school, and the 130 boy pupils, in their distinctive school attire, were a familiar part of the scene. In 1909, a 'sister' school was built in Fox Lane with Mrs. Temblett-Wood as Principal. This school also acted as a boys' preparatory school, in liaison with the Collegiate. Both schools set high standards and earned good reputations.

With the establishment of a strong state education system during this century, the number of private schools has gradually dwindled but they still have an important role to fulfil. The Collegiate School in Winchmore Hill closed in 1963.

The mansion of Fords Grove stood where Capitol House and the National Westminster Bank stands today. There was a brick wall along the Green Lanes frontage and the mansion, set in very extensive grounds, faced east across the New River* to the spinney and the more open aspect of, what is now, the Paulin Ground of Winchmore Hill Cricket Club.

Until 1889, it was the home of the Busk family. It was in 1720 that Merry Teshmaker purchased Fords Grove, to be followed by Thomas Teshmaker J.P., Lord of the Manor of Edmonton. He had a daughter Sarah who, in 1800, married Edward Busk. The Busk family were of Scandinavian origin, mostly merchants and lawyers, who had come to settle in England during the latter part of the 17th century. Edward was a barrister-at-law and had lived near Bedford Row but, soon after his marriage to Sarah, Mrs. Teshmaker, widow of Thomas, vacated the premises and moved to another part of Winchmore Hill.

Fords Grove then became the family home of Edward and Sarah Busk where their first son, Edward Thomas, was born in 1805. Edward Thomas married in 1851 and there were five children of this

*The private footbridge (recently extensively repaired) that led from the mansion across the New River still exists today and can be seen from the bridge in Fords Grove or, with more safety, from the car park of Capitol House.

union, of whom Thomas Teshmaker Busk, born in 1852, was the eldest son. Thus the two family names were perpetuated. 'T.T.B.', a barrister like his father, was appointed as J.P. for the county of Middlesex in 1883 and was the last of the Busks to live in Fords Grove, latterly with his wife and family.

The Busk family was held in the highest esteem by all sections of the community in Winchmore Hill and the surrounding areas. This goodwill was to continue long after their departure. 'T.T.B.' married Mary Acworth of Northaw in 1885 but, in 1889, they decided to move to 'Hermongers' in Rudgwick, Sussex, together with their two children, Edward and Mary. Mrs. Busk was a fine painter of water colours and, in later life, she kindly presented two of her local scenes to Southgate Museum.

Thomas Teshmaker Busk was to survive for only another 5 years, for he died in 1894 at the early age of 42. The family retained ownership of the Fords Grove estate, the son Edward* becoming landlord on his coming-of-age in 1907.

Winchmore Hill Village Cricket Club had been founded in 1880 when John Moore, head gardener to the Busk family at Fords Grove, had approached his master 'T.T.B.' for permission to play cricket in his private park, on the Firs Lane side of the existing ground. The relationship between the Club and the Busks began on a most friendly and cordial basis, which continued through future generations. I write more about the Cricket Club in Chapter 8.

Following the Busk family's move to Sussex in 1889, the residence was occupied by various tenants until 1903, when it fell vacant. The mansion became more and more dilapidated and was finally demolished in 1920.

Today, the site is taken up by Capitol House, a modern glass office block occupied by the Inland Revenue, together with the National Westminster Bank on the corner. There is a 30 year story to unfold, however, before we move on and it is a pleasure to tell it.

The research and the interviews, the long and painstaking hours spent transferring one's knowledge and thoughts into words, all adds up to a labour of love, really, but never more so than when the spotlight falls on our old cinemas. The reason is, I suppose, that I have lived through the halcyon days of movie entertainment and seen it all for myself. Many of my readers will have their own cinema memories of this period, which is why the feelings of nostalgia are so strong and so meaningful to us all.

*Edward T. Busk was a pioneer aviator and a test pilot at the Royal Aircraft Factory at Farnborough. He was killed in a flying accident in November 1914.

'Going to the flics' was part of our lives and a very important part at that. Once, twice or three times a week we would escape into another world as our favourite stars played havoc with our emotions and took us into new realms of fantasy. As I wrote in my Palmers Green book, it was a world of magic.

The stars of the silent screen were already worshipped and adored. It was plain that in 1927/28, with the added dimension of sound, the public's appetite would continue to grow. Some of the old cinemas experienced difficulty in raising the capital to invest in the new sound equipment required for the 'talkies.' Some liked to believe that it was a retrograde step anyway. The Alcazar in Fore Street, Edmonton, billed itself as 'The Silent House' – 'Speech is Silvern, but Silence is Golden.' It was not until the end of 1933, when the Alcazar was rebuilt, that sound facilities were introduced there.

The Capitol, 'specially designed for talking films' and 'the most luxurious theatre yet conceived', opened on Boxing Day 1929 with a seating capacity of 2,500 all told – 1,450 in the stalls and 1,050 in the circle or 'balcony' as it was called. It was correctly described as a 'theatre' in those early days for it served a dual role in offering talking pictures and a stage show, not to mention a fine orchestra and organ music thrown in for good measure.

What did the Capitol have to offer on its first bill of fare? A film entitled 'Twin Beds' with Jack Mulhall (talking, singing and dancing!) for the first 3 days, to be followed by 'The Idle Rich' with Conrad Nagel and Bessie Love. Performing on stage were Parr & Parr, the 'different' dancers, Rossland Chard, the celebrated vocalist, and 'The Eight Capitol Marshmallow Girls' in various novelty dances. Were they the Tiller girls of the future? I just wonder if any of the Marshmallows still survive?

There was a 20 piece orchestra under the direction of Sidney Shinbourne, plus a recital played on the huge John Compton organ that had been installed. The prices of admission were 6d, 9d, 1/-, 1/3 and 1/6 (stalls) and 1/6, 2/- (balcony) and the theatre opened at 1.30pm, first performance 2pm. There was a large cafe upstairs adjoining the circle, pure fresh air at an even temperature and the whole theatre was beautifully decorated in the Egyptian style. There was even a car park. Enough of the publicity notices, what about reality?

It really *was* a cinema of great appeal. I remember it so well because it was, by tradition, the family's place of entertainment every Monday evening, come what may. Occasionally, during periods in the blitz when Dad was on call, we would be depleted in numbers but otherwise, those of us who could make it, would be there. It was purely a cinema by this time, of course, though I do remember occasional stage acts and some local talent contests being held in the interval.

For the price of admission you got two good films, a news-reel, the trailers, a feature film, and some fine organ music. It comprised 3 hours of solid entertainment, interrupted only by a break for an ice cream tub or a choc ice. We always went in the 'one and nines', the centre stalls, on the right hand side if we could. Sometimes we would have to queue, even though Monday was recognised as a 'quiet' night.

We occasionally visited the cafe, a great place for afternoon tea. You had to climb the plush, carpeted stairs and pass the massive portraits of the great film stars of the day. I can close my eyes now and vividly recall those portraits of Clark Gable, Hedy Lamarr and Claudette Colbert.

2,500 seats would indicate a large cinema. It was and yet, in my experience, it had an intimate, friendly atmosphere and of course, its own special fragrance. Readers may smile, for I have mentioned it before in my previous books, but I can still recapture those subtle hints of haunting aromas that played round our nostrils, each cinema with its own speciality.

The Capitol became an ABC circuit cinema, with a first class weekly programme, the same as normally shown at the Ritz in Bowes Road. After the war, in common with most cinemas, the attendances started to decline. It was the growth of home viewing of the smaller screen that caused it, plus a complete change in our social habits. In our area the Capitol (1959) was an early casualty followed by the Palmadium (1961), the Queens (1967), the Odeon (1972) and the Ritz (1974).

The Capitol had shut temporarily in February 1958, the high entertainment tax, imposed at that time, being blamed. This was reduced in a subsequent budget and, to public acclaim, the cinema was reopened 11 weeks later. Alas, the stay of execution was short and, the following year, at very short notice, the cinema closed its doors for the last time on 5th December 1959. The final programme was 'The Man Who Could Cheat Death' with Christopher Lee and Hazel Court and 'The Evil that is Eve' with Mylene Demongeot. We all stood to attention as the National Anthem was played for the very last time.

The Capitol had served the public for 30 years and given pleasure to millions. I hope these few words have enabled you to recall your own special memories and some of that pleasure.

Between Station Road and Radcliffe Road, the houses show few signs of scars now, but I do recall a scene of destruction etched on a young boy's mind at the time, when a bomb was dropped here during the air raids.

We pass Radcliffe Road, named after a Doctor Samuel Radcliffe (1580-1648), Principal of Brasenose College, Oxford, who built a school at Steeple Aston in the early 1630's. He owned land in Winchmore Hill, in this vicinity, and donated most of the rents to augment his school's income.

Beyond Berry Close, there are some unusual-looking commercial properties. A pair of gates, with numbers 843 and 845 marked on the piers, give access to a yard. Many of us will remember these premises serving their original purpose, as the stables and depot of Stapletons Dairies.

On the other side of the road is Winchmore Hill Garage, with its extensive workshops behind, that continues to serve us well. Frederick John Rudling came from Stamford Hill in 1926/27 to set up the business and it has remained very much a family concern ever since. Frederick G. Rudling (son of F.J.) is now the Managing Director. He and his wife were kind enough to invite me to their home 'Riverside', built next to the garage, where we spoke about the early days of Winchmore Hill.

During the last war, the garage was commandeered as Meat Depot, number 7. Smithfield market was considered too vulnerable to air raid attack and depots were dispersed around London to minimise the risk. The petrol pumps fell idle and, under Fred's direction, a workshop and munitions factory was set up, turning out vital components to help the war effort. It was all a question of priorities in those days.

I glanced at their lovely garden, backing on to the New River, and bade them goodbye. The garage was doing a brisk trade and, as I tried to cross the Green Lanes, the traffic was continuous and never-ending. Winchmore Hill Garage has witnessed so many changes during its 64 years life span.

Next door, between the garage and the back gardens of Elm Park Road, lies Century House. Rowley Brothers, building contractors, had built extensively in the Tottenham area and, when Mr. Robert Rowley came to live in Winchmore Hill, he so named this house, being the hundredth his company had completed. The family remained there until 1971, when the Southgate Conservative Association took it over.

The stretch of Green Lanes between Station Road and Vicars

Moor Lane is an interesting one. For two centuries or more, it was known as Man's Lane and shows thus on some of the old maps. The name is derived from Edward Man, a London bookseller, whose country home, dating from the middle of the 17th century, was at Ford Green.

The exact position is difficult to define, because Green Lanes then was still a comparatively narrow track. The subsequent road widening, plus the creation of new roads, has encroached and made identification difficult. Ford Green was an open green, immediately west of the New River, near today's junctions of Fords Grove, Farm Road, Queens Avenue and Green Lanes. In my researches, I have never seen a picture or a description of Edward Man's house and its precise position has never been determined.

We do know a little about the gentleman, however, for he was an early Quaker and friend of George Fox, founder of the Society of Friends. We know that Fox came to Winchmore Hill in March 1681, and on various subsequent occasions. Each time, he would stay with his friend Edward Man at Ford Green. Man owned land along the Green Lanes, including a little row of cottages situated where the shops are today, immediately south of Shrubbery Gardens.

These were sometime later demolished and replaced by a row of 6 charming weather-boarded dwellings known as Busk's Cottages, from the family who then owned them, the Busks of Fords Grove. Some of my readers may recall them, as they were demolished around 1933. They were tiny little places, each no more than 10 or 11 feet wide. The entrance doors were in pairs with just two small sash windows in the front elevation to each cottage, one downstairs and one upstairs. The roof was pierced by chimney stacks and had a short, steep slope at the front and a long, raking slope to the rear. The tiny front gardens were bright with flowers confined by a picket fence and tiny entrance gates.

It is as well to reflect on this section of Green Lanes before the turn of the century. The highway of today bears little comparison with that of a hundred years ago. Today's road surface is 40 feet wide. Near Shrubbery Gardens, there is a 20 feet wide pavement on the west side and a 10 feet wide pavement on the east side.

Prior to the coming of the trams, the road surface was a mere 26 feet wide, with a raised gravelled footpath about 4 feet wide on the western side only. There was no gutter, merely a 3 feet long kerbstone placed every 8 or 10 yards. On the eastern side of the road was a sloping grass bank, about 18 inches wide, and then trees.

Opposite Busks' Cottages was a long row of tall stately elms, closely planted, in the grounds of Beaulieu, a beautifully timbered

Busks' Cottages have been replaced by shops.

Beaulieu, set in a beautiful wooded estate, eventually fell to the developers.

The top picture shows the second Green Dragon inn, built in the 1780's. The middle photograph shows how narrow the Green Lanes used to be, and the bottom one reveals the coming of the trams and the widening of the roadway.

estate from the bank of the New River to Green Lanes. Elm Park Road was not cut through until 1898/9. In those days, the Green Lanes turned eastwards in a sharp 90° bend in front of the Green Dragon, with the lodge to Beaulieu on the opposite corner.

The widening of this section of Green Lanes, in 1907, to prepare for the coming of the trams, involved the felling of the elms and the construction of the great curve in the road, to replace the awkward right angle that preceded it.

The old Beaulieu estate thus lost its lodge and a considerable area on the corner, plus a strip of land more than 20 feet wide on the Green Lanes frontage, opposite the cottages. This involved the loss of many beautiful elm trees, that once lined the Green Lanes in profusion, right round to the northern end of Firs Lane. It also meant that No.2. Elm Park Road had a considerable section sliced off, to accommodate the widened roadway. The pebbledashed flank wall facing Green Lanes is not the original.

Let us take a closer look at Beaulieu. Its position is best pinpointed by the road now called Beaulieu Gardens, where the mansion stood close by the New River in the most beautiful surroundings. The River is particularly appealing along this section, as it winds its way through attractive grounds in a delightful setting. This can still be appreciated today, if we take a stroll and glance through the shrubs into the garden between numbers 9 and 10. What must it have been like before its demise?

The well-timbered grounds were bounded in the south by Squire Busk's estate of Fords Grove, i.e. the southern boundary ran from the rear of No.2 Elm Park Road easterly to meet the New River, then along the river's course as far as the bridge in Firs Lane. The perimeter elsewhere was marked by Green Lanes and Firs Lane. The size of the estate, just over 10 acres, was eroded by the cutting through of Elm Park Road, and the subsequent road widening of the Green Lanes I have already described.

The grounds were densely wooded with some magnificent specimen trees. Before the development, the whole area remained as nature had intended, a haven of peace little disturbed by man. It became a sanctuary for many species of birds and wildlife that made Beaulieu their home. Owls, jackdaws, nightingales, crows, red squirrels and many other creatures enjoyed the natural habitat. In March 1900, Oliver G. Pike, FRPS, FZS, published his book 'In Birdland with Field-glass and Camera' which was illustrated with photographs taken at Beaulieu.

Beaulieu is thought to have been built towards the end of the 18th century for John Gray, brother of Walker Gray, for whom John Nash and Humphry Repton created the mansion and park we know today as Grovelands, later to become the home of the Taylors. John Gray sold out to Thomas Nisbett.

We know little of John Gray or Thomas Nisbett, but we do know more of the renowned Cass family of East Barnet who followed. In 1806, William Cass purchased the estate for £4,750 which, on his death, was handed down to his son Frederick. He was a highly respected man, later to be appointed High Sherrif for Hertfordshire. The Reverend Frederick Charles Cass, son of Frederick, was born at Beaulieu in 1824 and moved to Littlegrove in Cat Hill with his parents in 1827. F.C. Cass wrote several books on local history including The History of South Mimms (1877), Monken Hadley (1880), and East Barnet (1885). He was Rector of Monken Hadley from 1860 to 1890.

Thomas Paulin and his family moved into Beaulieu in 1865 for a stay of 8 years. His son, William Thomas Paulin, grew into manhood here before his move to Broadfields, which he built on the site of a small farm off Wades Hill. W.T. Paulin and his family were to have a major influence on Winchmore Hill affairs which I have outlined in Chapters 4 and 8. Subsequently, the Phillips family resided at Beaulieu and, in 1892, the East Window of St. Pauls was erected in memory of Lewis and Jane Phillips of Beaulieu by their family.

Towards the end of the 19th century, it was purchased by Mr. Foster of Palfreyman, Foster & Co., renowned timber importers. Mr. Foster cut Elm Park Road through the estate in 1898/9 and development soon followed. Alfred Hicklin was the builder of most of the properties in the new road and also the shops, numbers 820 to 844 (from Elm Park Road to the corner), in the much widened Green Lanes.

For a few years, at the beginning of this century, Beaulieu became a boarding school for ladies, then followed two unsuccessful attempts to run it as a private residential hotel. In 1910, it was offered to the Council for £4,000, but the offer was refused. The Council, at this time, was negotiating with Capt. J.V. Taylor over Grovelands and there were no surplus funds available.

At the outbreak of war in 1914, the mansion was empty and it was commandeered for the housing of Belgian refugees. Much sterling work was done by the committee, set up to make them feel at home. It was during this period that the great gale of 1916 wrought havoc with our trees, and Beaulieu did not go unscathed. Eventually, in 1919, came repatriation and Beaulieu was empty once more.

The house was too large to attract local buyers. The days of the landed gentry were over. Commercial enterprise had already been tried and had failed. In one last move to make it viable, the uppermost storey was demolished in 1922, a new roof provided and maintenance work carried out, but it was all in vain. Beaulieu lingered on, a sorry sight, a survivor from a forgotten age, until relief came with its demolition in 1937.

One house called The Shrubbery stood alone on the western side of Green Lanes, just before Vicars Moor Lane, and is worthy of mention for, miraculously, it has survived, though in a completely different form from the original. The detached house once stood in 4 acres of ground, a charming ivy-covered old place. I have a picture showing the south or garden front, which has now been built upon.

In 1926/7, the house was simply absorbed into a parade of shops and is today (1989) the Dragon Garden Chinese Restaurant and Sterns Chemists. The shop fronts are continuous but, if we stand back, we can identify the house which, at first floor level, remains detached from the adjacent premises. Shrubbery Gardens, which cuts through the grounds, perpetuates the name.

I should not have realised the significance of The Shrubbery, except that I am privileged to know the dear lady who, as a child, once lived there and was able to tell me something of its past. Her name is Dorothy Cole (nee Kynaston). Her parents rented the house for some years, from 1911 onwards, when it stood alone in its own grounds. Her vivid memory is of looking through her bedroom windows to watch the trams go by. That room and its windows, fronting Green Lanes, are still there. She also has a clear recollection of playing with her chums in the fields at the back and coming out into a quiet lane, where the vicar once had his well. After all these years, 'Auntie' Dorothy can still recall the happy times of her childhood.

Vicars Moor Lane was once called Front Lane, (Station Road was Middle Lane and Compton Road was Back Lane). Following the sinking of a well by the Vicar of Edmonton early in the 18th century, to give his parishioners on the moor a readily available water supply, the present name came into being. The site of the well was in front of, what is now, the garage to number 12 Pritchett Terrace (41 Vicars Moor Lane) and nearby was the rear entrance into the grounds of The Shrubbery.

In carrying out more research, I learned that the house, which originally stood on the site, was enlarged to greater proportions by a Mr. G.L. Warner, an accomplished artist who built a studio in the grounds. The Shrubbery was tenanted from 1906 to 1911 by Colonel Arthur Willis M.B.E., J.P. who, in a very busy and full life, still found the time to become one of our most respected local historians.

Arthur Willis (1858-1942) was born in Sheffield and married Catherine in 1883. They moved to North London and often stayed with their friends, the Metherells*, at Elmscott in Bush Hill. He became President of the Winchmore Hill Ratepayers Association in 1904 and a Southgate Councillor in 1907. This was just the start of a long and full life in public service, in many different spheres, for the list is endless.

Arthur served on many committees in various capacities and always applied himself with a dedication that became his hallmark. Even so, he found the time to write on a subject dear to him, local history. Under the pen name of 'Topical' and later 'Memorabilia', he wrote regularly for the Palmers Green Gazette. His research was always thorough and reliable. He sought to be accurate, down to the smallest detail, and one sensed an underlying love of the area that had become his home.

He moved into Elm Lodge, part of which is now 2 Elm Park Road, and later moved to number 20†. Colonel Willis was awarded the M.B.E. in the First World War for his work in connection with the Ministry of Munitions. As a J.P., he sat for many years at the Wood Green, Enfield and Tottenham Courthouses. In 1941, Southgate Borough Council conferred on him the Honorary Freedom of the Borough, but he died in the following September, 1942, active to the very end of his 84 years.

There were many others who contributed but, in their different styles, Henrietta Cresswell, Arthur Willis, Tom Mason, Herbert Newby and Horace Regnart were paramount in recording our past, whilst still being aware of the changes taking place during their own lifetimes.

As we reach the Green Dragon Hotel, the Green Lanes turns abruptly to the right and we pass the junction with Firs Lane. On the near corner is Firs Hall, a long established venue for ballroom dancing, which many of us will remember from our youth. With the gradual decline in popularity of dancing, the hall has been taken over by a well-established catering firm and has changed its role

*Richard Metherell & Son were responsible for the setting out and development of the Grange Park area.
†Numbers 20 & 22 Elm Park Road have disappeared with the building of Blenheim Close.

into a high class banqueting suite, renamed The Firs.

On the other corner with Firs Lane, now occupied by the Telephone Exchange built in 1937, there once stood the Gibraltar Cottages. The origin of the name is interesting. It is generally accepted that they were built in the 1780's by John Blackburn, a major landowner, who lived at Bush Hill House, now known as the Halliwick Home. Mr. Blackburn (1731-1798) was the contractor responsible for supplying food to our garrison in Gibraltar, including during the difficult years of siege imposed by the combined Spanish and French forces (1779-1783), and he named the cottages accordingly.

They are part of a delightful scene in the old photographs showing a narrow tree-lined Green Lanes, a grassed triangle at the entrance to Firs Lane on which is a lamp illuminating an old fashioned signpost, and a picket fence bordering the corner in a big arc, with graceful trees abounding. The corner cottage was used at one time as a posting and receiving office for the mail. Deliveries were made twice daily and the letters would then await collection by the addressees. When it was demolished, there was evidence revealed of a postal aperture in the wall on the Green Lanes side and a cavity in the wall, acting as the post box.

The corner field had once been known as Tile Barrow Field, confirming the presence in the district (to which any gardener will concur) of considerable deposits of clay suitable for the making of bricks and tiles. There was still evidence of the old clay pit excavations to be seen in the early years of this century, though production would have ceased prior to 1800.

As late as 1907, the occupier of the larger of the two cottages did a thriving trade in bouquets and button holes of choice flowers to passers-by, especially on Saturday afternoons and Sundays, for the district was then a favourite drive for London publicans. They delighted to rival each other in friendly matches, with their fast trotting ponies and sporty looking dog carts and gigs, which they drove at full speed usually along the Green Lanes, from the Manor House to the Green Dragon.

The Green Dragon that we know today is the third inn of that name and the second on the present site. The original Green Dragon was situated at, what later became known as, Masons Corner, i.e. at the extreme western end of Ridge Avenue, opposite the eastern end of Green Dragon Lane. This explains the naming of the lane and why today the pub and the lane are remote from each other.

The original licence is thought to date from the early 18th century and legend has it that there used to be a gallows positioned near the front of the inn. The spot was reputed to be notorious for robberies by highwaymen and footpads, defenceless villagers being frequently accosted in Bush Hill on either side of the brook, where it flows under the New River. The villains could lie in wait here, unseen, and spring out on to their unsuspecting victims.

In 1753, the postman on his way from Edmonton to Winchmore Hill was murdered and robbed by two youths aged 17 and 20, at the junction of Green Dragon Lane and Bush Hill. They were both sentenced to death and executed. As was customary in those days their bodies, dressed in the clothes they wore when they committed the murder, were brought to Winchmore Hill and hung up in chains on the gallows close to the inn. Another highwayman, arrested in the bar of the Green Dragon in 1780, met a similar fate. The bodies would be left there for several months, as a deterrent to other would-be offenders. The gruesome sight, together with the bad reputation of the area, had an adverse affect on trade and, in the 1780's, the landlord decided to move to a new inn built at the bottom of Vicars Moor Lane, where it remained for more than a century. It was demolished in 1893, to make way for the present building, built slightly to the west of the one it replaced.

After the first inn was vacated, the building was taken over by Mr. Blackburn, who converted it into a lodge for his estate and it remained so, until Ridge Avenue was made in 1907. When it was pulled down, the basement was found to contain an extensive cellarage. The old inn was in close proximity to a field known as Dead Field. This was the area where the Edmonton victims of the plague shared a common grave in the 1660's. Dead Field is today covered by Percy Road, Solna Road, Kent Road and Colne Road.

I have never seen a picture of the first Green Dragon, but there is a photograph of the second in existence, plus a sketch drawn by Doctor Cresswell. It was a plain Georgian building with imitation marble pillars featured at the entrance, supporting a small portico roof which served a useful purpose for the genteel ladies of Winchmore Hill when they boarded the stage-coach. It was considered indelicate to expose their ankles when mounting to the top seats by means of a ladder. Instead, the landlord allowed them to climb the stairs in his domestic quarters and board the coach from the portico roof.

The Inn had excellent stabling facilities and a long open shed with a manger, in which the customers could tie up their horses. The coaches, which started from the Green Dragon, went from

The Green Dragon of the late 1920's *(top)*
compared with today's appearance *(lower)*.
Apart from the style of motor car, can you spot the many differences?

The delighful Gibraltar Cottages, built by John Blackburn in the 1780's, stood on the corner of Firs Lane.

Tile Barrow Field and the cottages have given way to modern development and the Telephone Exchange.

Winchmore Hill to London Bridge, via the Green Lanes and Wood Green. They would be pulled by three horses and the journey took nearly 2 hours.

The second inn, like the first, was also used for many years as a posting and receiving station. When the mail coach passed by in the early hours of the morning, the landlord would stir from his sleep to throw the mail bags on to the top of the coach, from the bedroom window. The story goes that one morning, after a night of much revelry and in a semi-conscious state, he threw out his leather breeches by mistake. On waking up late, he was alarmed to find the mailbags at the foot of the bed, instead of his breeches.

Throughout its early history, the Green Dragon was a very popular venue for a day out in the country. The inner populace of the metropolis would come by horsebus to quench their thirst with the good ale and fill their lungs with the fresh air north of London. The Inn had a reputation for its skittles alley and the great contests held there. On occasions, crowds would gather to lay their bets at the cock-fighting.

The new Green Dragon Hotel, built in 1893, was in complete contrast to the modest plain edifice that preceded it. At the time, it was considered to be a building of exceptional quality, style and design.* Many thought it a somewhat ambitious project creating, as it did, a rather grand hotel in this lovely country village of Winchmore Hill. The design inspired an article in the Building News of 17th February 1893, extolling its virtues and including a fine illustration of the new Hotel, showing a stagecoach approaching along a Green Lanes that still lived up to its name.

In 1907, the tramway extension from Manor House was opened. The 'end of the ride' then was the Green Dragon. In the winter of 1908, work commenced on the final stretch of track, a 1¾ mile stretch into Enfield Town. As originally proposed, soon after leaving the Inn, the line would have to scale the steep slope of Bush Hill, go past the gates of Old Park (now the golf course) and join the present London Road near Uvedale Road.

The gradient in Bush Hill was the problem. However, as a result of negotiation with the owners of the Red Ridge estate, a new 60 ft. road (Ridge Avenue) was cut from the foot of Green Dragon Lane, to run eastwards towards Village Road, joining with Park Avenue, before turning into London Road on its way to Enfield Town. In

*The architect was George Skipper of Norwich. He built some fine seaside hotels at Cromer, Yarmouth and Lowestoft, and the Norwich Union offices at Norwich.

this way, the hill was avoided and the main route into Enfield completely altered.

The flags and the bunting were out on that July day in 1909, when the new extension was opened and the first tram left Enfield by the George Inn. Crowds lined the route all the way to Winchmore Hill. The trams were already running from Ponders End into Enfield along Southbury Road, and there were plans to connect up the two systems at the junctions. This was never done, as it proved too expensive a business to widen the old bottleneck, which constricted Southbury Road at the Town end. The widening here did not come until the 1930's, with the demise of the Nags Head.

The arrival of the tramway in 1907/09 was a very important forerunner to the development of the whole area, and reinforced the Green Lanes as one of the main arteries leading into and out of London.

The mention of Masons Corner reminds me that I cannot leave without due reference to the store (now occupied by Days Cycles) which gave its name to the area. It was one of those fine hardware shops that are fast becoming extinct. Mr. Mason himself will be remembered by many reading these pages, as a man striving to give good service in that friendly, helpful manner he always adopted.

And so we have come to the northern extremity of Green Lanes, a road that starts its life today at Newington Green, and continues its 7 mile journey through the suburbs. The cattle are no longer shepherded along its route as in days of yore. Change was slow and gradual until the turn of the century, since when it has been transformed into a major highway.

The Lanes are green no more but they have played, and continue to play, an important role in the history and development of our region.

# CHAPTER 7

## BUSH HILL AND THE NEW RIVER

AT MASONS CORNER all the traffic swings right and travels eastwards into Ridge Avenue on its way to Enfield. Though the shops peter out, it appears to be a continuation of the main road, albeit in a changed direction and under a different name. We are unaware that we have come to a parting of the ways.

For centuries, the way north to Enfield continued along by the New River, up the incline of Bush Hill and onwards. It was then still known as Green Lanes. The vast Old Park estate stretched away to the west, as far as Worlds End Lane and all around we could enjoy the glorious, wooded countryside. Past Carrs Lane (once the carriage approach to a house called Chase Park) we would start to descend, crossing the New River to join London Road where the limit of our region is reached, some half a mile short of Enfield Town.

The arrival of the trams caused the route to be changed. It was realised that the gradients of Bush Hill would be too steep to negotiate, and Ridge Avenue was constructed, in 1907, to link up with Village Road and Park Avenue where London Road could be rejoined. In more recent times we have witnessed the final act, with the closing of Bush Hill at its southern end to prevent any traffic using, what had been at one time, the main route through to Enfield.

This is an appropriate place to write about the New River in some detail for here, running parallel to Bush Hill, is a section of the canal (for it is not a river) that caused special problems during its construction, 1609-1613. There were great design and engineering skills required in building the large aqueduct to span the valley, taking the river across and above Salmons Brook.

I have long been interested in the New River. It is one of those subjects where the more you research, the more committed you become, as you realise what a great example of man's endeavours and ingenuity it was, and still remains to this day.

In 1600, during the reign of Queen Elizabeth I, London was a city of some 180,000 inhabitants. The chief source of water supply was the River Thames and its tributaries, spring-fed conduits and individual wells. Those city dwellers not close to one of these sources had to rely on the water carrier. He was, indeed, a familiar sight, carrying a wooden yoke across his shoulders from which two wooden barrel-shaped buckets were suspended, one either side.

Londoners continued to use the River Thames indiscriminately as a convenient dumping place for rubbish and for sewage disposal. The city was expanding and, with many of the original sources becoming contaminated and a serious risk to health, there was an urgent need for a fresh water supply to be introduced.

In 1570, an Act of Parliament authorised the construction of a river within 10 years, to bring water to the high ground north of the city, whence it could be gravity fed in pipes to the built up areas. The Act lapsed with nothing achieved until 1600, when Edmund Colthurst proposed that a channel be dug along the 100 ft. contour from the springs of Amwell and Chadwell, near Hertford, to Islington. Although the scheme had the blessing of the Queen, she died before the licence could be granted. In 1604, King James I authorised the work to proceed but, when Colthurst appealed for financial support having spent £200 of his own money in starting the project, the City Corporation decided instead to promote a new bill in 1606, using Colthurst's scheme as the basis. In March 1609, the Corporation accepted an offer by Hugh Myddelton to complete the work in four years.

Hugh Myddelton, born in 1560, was the sixth son of Richard Myddelton, Governor of Denbigh Castle. He had travelled from North Wales to London, at the age of 16, to serve his goldsmith's apprenticeship and had proved successful in the trade. He was appointed as an Alderman of Denbigh and represented that borough in Parliament. Myddelton became one of the Merchant Adventurers of England, his earliest engineering enterprise having been in coal mining near Denbigh about 1600.

The New River was a marvellous conception, years ahead of its time. The canal would follow the 100 ft. contour so that, although the distance from the Hertford springs to New River Head in Islington was 24 miles, the channel needed to be cut was nearly 40 miles long. There were some lengthy loops in the course of the river, passing up one side of a valley and back down the other. The total fall from start to finish was only 18 feet, an average of 5½" per mile, so one can appreciate the precision required and, remember, this was nearly 400 years ago.

The project met with considerable opposition, even ridicule, and then ran into serious financial difficulties. King James I, who knew Myddelton, allowed the New River to be cut through the Royal estates at Theobalds free of charge and agreed to provide half the cost of the total undertaking, on condition that he would receive half the profits. King James is reputed to have seldom washed and to have been averse to water, both as a drink and a means of cleanliness. A keen but clumsy horseman, he was involved in an accident in his grounds when, to quote the writer of the time:-

'His horse stumbled and cast his Majesty into the New River, where the ice broke. Sir Richard Young was next, who alighted, went into the water, and lifted him out. There came much water out of his mouth and body. His Majesty rode back to Theobalds, went into a warm bed and, as we hear, is well which God continue.'

It was at this time that the major undertaking of the Bush Hill aqueduct had to be faced. Here, the New River was carried across the valley and above Salmons Brook in a wooden trough lined with lead. The trough, 6 feet wide and 5 feet deep, was 660 feet long and originally supported on massive timber arches reaching a height of 24 feet. Myddelton was very much on hand to supervise these works as he had acquired, and was living in, his country residence, Bush Hill House, through the grounds of which the aqueduct was to flow. Bush Hill House, much altered and enlarged, was later to become the Halliwick Home.

In the N21 area, the New River flows southwards under Ridge Avenue, then behind houses and under the hump-backed bridge in Firs Lane. It continues along the western side of Winchmore Hill cricket ground, behind Green Lanes, and under two more narrow bridges in Fords Grove and Farm Road. It soon emerges to run parallel to Green Lanes, crossed by more hump-backed bridges in Highfield Road, Carpenter Gardens and Barrowell Green. We can still see the old pumping station, now obsolete, on the north side of the bridge in Carpenter Gardens.

Much further south, in Palmers Green, a massive loop had to be dug starting just by the present Southgate Town Hall. The river here originally ran westwards, just to the south of Dawlish Avenue (then just open fields) across what is now Arnos Park, to cross Pymmes Brook just before the bridge in Waterfall Lane. It then returned to flow eastwards on the northern side of Bowes Road, between Pymmes Brook and the road. This was immediately followed by another large loop to the east, towards Edmonton.

And so the work went ahead with, it is said, some 600 labourers earning half-a-crown per day. The original concept required 157 bridges to be built over the flowing water and the total cost of the project was half a million pounds. The great day arrived. In spite of all the difficulties, constructional and financial, which had caused some delays and, notwithstanding the opposition shown by some of the landowners, the great enterprise neared completion. The work had started in April 1609 and now, less than 4½ years later, all was ready. On 29th September 1613, the floodgates were opened and 'the sweet waters of Hertfordshire flowed into the Round Pond at New River Head'.

A similar scheme today would present a daunting challenge. In 1609, without mechanisation and the earth moving equipment we now possess, it was a remarkable achievement and a lasting tribute to all who took part.

The water was distributed along the streets of London in pipes made from elm tree trunks. These had been bored out with a central hole of up to 7″ diameter. The end of each 'pipe' was sharpened like a pencil and driven into the tapered bore of the next. It may seem crude, but it was effective.

I remember that my father, in course of business, had come across some of these old elm pipes. They had come to light during excavation work on a building site. He had a slice, about 3″ thick, cut off and beautifully polished. He then fixed a mirror backing over the hole with two hat and coat hooks screwed to the face. As a boy, I remember it hanging in his office for years. I wonder what became of it? Cast iron pipes were not introduced until 1793, when they gradually replaced the old elm tree trunks.

Since the opening in 1613, there have been major alterations to the New River and its function. Within 50 years, the flow from the springs proved inadequate and water was diverted from the River Lee. This caused a great deal of protest from the mill owners, who relied on the Lee to drive their waterwheels. The bargemen, too, were not happy, for they depended on a full flowing river for good navigation in their trade with London. An Act of Parliament ordered careful monitoring and control, by means of a gauge, of the volume of water allowed to flow from the Lee into the New River, so that the river's flow should not become too depleted.

I find it most interesting when, from time to time, our local history impinges upon matters of more national importance. The research takes on a wider aspect and gives us a sense of proportion. Such was the case towards the end of the 18th century, when the Gordon riots began in earnest. The riots were caused by the strong anti-Catholic feelings which existed at the time. The Government had proposed that certain restrictions imposed on the Catholics should be lifted.

Lord George Gordon (1751-93) led the movement in opposition

Bush Hill House, now Halliwick College, once the home of Sir Hugh Myddelton, prime motivator of the New River.

The construction of the New River (1609-13) was a remarkable achievement. Here we see the aqueduct that crosses Salmons Brook.

Sir Hugh Myddelton saw little financial reward for his great endeavours.

Bush Hill from the Enfield end, looking south, showing the road bridge over the New River.

to the Government's proposals and a meeting of his followers, in 1780, was followed by indiscriminate damage to property in London. The guards were called out, but the rioters held London for a fortnight, such was their strength of purpose. It was during that fortnight, in July 1780, that the rioters threatened to destroy the Bush Hill aqueduct, thus cutting off London's water supply. The New River Company appealed to the Government for military protection and two regiments were sent for urgent guard duties.

The riots subsided and normality was restored, but the troops remained. It is thought they may have been billeted in Winchmore Hill, or possibly they lived in a tented encampment on Pike's fields, amongst the orchards. As autumn approached it was clear that, by now, the soldiers had outstayed their welcome but, for some reason, the military authorities were reluctant to order their withdrawal. Whilst praising the behaviour of the officers and men, the New River Company appealed several times in the strongest of terms that, with danger now averted, the military presence was no longer required. The soldiers left on 20th October 1780.

Lord George Gordon was committed to the Tower on a charge of treason, but was acquitted. In 1787, he was imprisoned in Newgate jail for libelling the British judiciary and died insane there, six years later.

At Bush Hill the aqueduct had been raised by one foot in 1725. In 1786, largely due to maintenance problems, the trough and its supports were replaced entirely by a clay bank. The old lead lining to the aqueduct, weighing nearly 50 tons, was sold to local plumbers at 18 shillings per ton.

The Clarendon Arch was built in 1682 to replace the old bridge in Bush Hill. It carries a coat of arms and the inscription 'This Arch was Rebuilt in the Yeare 1682, Honourable Henry Earle of Clarendon being Govr.'. The archway supports the road and originally carried the waters of Salmons Brook eastwards, under both the roadway and the New River. With permission, it may be possible to clamber down, as I did, on the west side to view the Arch which is obsolete today. The waters of Salmons Brook have been culverted in a massive concrete circular ducting some 7 feet in diameter just to the south, thus bypassing the Arch. The approaches are now dry and heavily buttressed with timbers on both sides. I went down the track leading to Hazelwood Lawn Tennis Club and beyond, to view the Arch on the east side of the New River and, after some days of heavy rain (February 1989), the brook was in full flow. The back gardens on the north side of Park Drive go down to the brook.

My wife and I lived in one of these houses (No. 11), nearly 40 years ago, and we vividly remember the scenes of extensive flooding that occurred during heavy rainstorms. The culvert has been built since then to relieve the problem.

As London continued to develop and expand during the latter half of the nineteenth century, so the demand for water grew ever larger. The New River Company began sinking wells, operated by steam pumps, along the River's course, whereby the fresh water could be pumped up from depths of up to 1,000 feet and fed into the main stream, thus augmenting the supply. No fewer than 12 such wells were sunk in the period 1847 to 1898 and brought into operation.

One of these, known as the Highfield Well and Pumping Station, was sunk in our region in 1885. This is situated on the north side of the Carpenter Gardens/Green Lanes junction, on the eastern bank of the New River, where the well depth was 371 feet. Many of us will recall the tall chimney that soared high into the sky, marking the site of the pumping station. It was a familiar local landmark but, when the pumps were switched to electric power, its useful life came to an end and it was demolished. The Highfield pumping station ceased to operate in 1962 though, at time of writing (March 1989), the fine old building remains, to remind us of a little part of history in our midst.

Many of the loops in the course of the canal have been made obsolete by the use of pipes, culverts and aqueducts, considerably shortening its length. The use of the Round Pond at New River Head ceased in 1914 and the surrounding filter beds were abandoned in 1945. The New River then terminated at the Stoke Newington reservoirs.

And so the changes continue. The latest plans of the Thames Water Authority include a complete reorganisation of London's water distribution. A ring main, 8 feet in diameter, is planned to encircle the capital, thus making the New River, south of Cheshunt, redundant as far as London's water supply is concerned. For environmental reasons, there are many conservationist groups and others pressing for its retention in some form. Let us hope they are successful.

We shall always be indebted to those early pioneers. Men like Colthurst, and later on the engineers Henry Mill, Robert Mylne and his son William Chadwell Mylne who made sure the system worked. Myddelton is usually recognised as the chief motivator. On 19th October 1622, he was created a baronet with the title of Sir Hugh

Myddelton of Ruthin in the county of Denbigh but, like many innovators, Sir Hugh did not live to see any great financial reward for his New River endeavours. Let us be proud that such a man once lived here in Winchmore Hill.

As we travel northwards in Bush Hill and come to the top of the rise, we come to a T-junction. Bush Hill continues to our left but we should linger awhile by turning right, where we can see the tiny Sluice House spanning the river on the north side of the bridge. There are several of these along the course of the River and their function, of course, is to allow control and regulation of the flow of water passing through. Until recent times, there was a house on the eastern bank of the river, immediately adjoining the Sluice House, which had been occupied from 1811 to 1861 by William Chadwell Mylne, Chief Engineer to the New River Company.

Opposite is the entrance to Halliwick College, once known as Bush Hill House. The Halliwick School, run by the Church of England Children's Society, was founded in 1851 and moved to Bush Hill in 1911, where it continued to provide a great service for disabled young people. A little elbow in the New River skirts the house once owned by Hugh Myddelton and his family nearly 400 years ago, whilst he was directing operations on the construction of the river and the nearby aqueduct in particular. What a scene of great activity it must have presented at that time.

The house has been much altered since Sir Hugh's time and it is uncertain how much of the original now remains. A blue plaque commemorates the great man. Later owners have included John Blackburn, who owned a great deal of land in the vicinity and who was the supplier of provisions to our garrison in Gibraltar. I have discussed this elsewhere.

The Currie family owned Bush Hill House for a long period. They were well-known bankers in the City and they set about recasing the house in brick and enlarging the residence considerably. Lord Currie (formerly Sir Philip Currie) was the owner of Old Park Grange, on whose death Richard Metherell purchased the estate in 1906. This triggered the subsequent development of Grange Park. The Curries made their mark locally and were liberal donors to the fund raised in 1827 for the building of St. Paul's Church in Winchmore Hill.

For 10 years (1850-1860) Bush Hill House was leased to Sir Samuel Cunard, the founder and owner of the great shipping line. He caused a stir locally by making a serious complaint and remonstrating with the Postmaster General about the morning delivery of his mail at Bush Hill, which was not arriving until 11 a.m. Thereafter the delivery was made promptly at 9 a.m.

The estate was duly broken up for development. Prior to Halliwick's occupation, the house was used for a time as a boarding school for girls.

North of Bush Hill Road, the border of our region runs very close to the east bank of the New River. The Orchard, Orchardmede, Ringmer Place, Quakers Walk and Bush Hill itself are very pleasant residential roads within the N21 district. They constitute a mere fraction of the 373 acres that were scheduled for development by the Bush Hill Park Estate Company in 1875, the greater part lying in Enfield, outside the London Postal Region. However, the area is a very interesting one and worth exploring. The houses vary greatly in their size, style and origin.

The name Quakers Walk is derived from a row of houses, once occupied by members of the Society of Friends (including some of the Barclay family) and named Quakers Row. They were demolished by Squire William Mellish of Bush Hill Park around 1825. Quakers had an early presence in our area with Meeting Houses in both Winchmore Hill and Enfield, from as early as 1688 and 1697, respectively.

Before any building work was undertaken, the developers sunk a well in Quakers Walk to provide a good water supply for the estate. A brick-built, covered reservoir holding 40,000 gallons was constructed alongside. A brick water tower was then built adjoining with a cast iron tank at high level giving an extra 40 feet of head, together with the necessary pumping plant. In this way a good water pressure would be assured.

The tower was never used for its original purpose for, when the New River Company bought up the works in 1887/8, they started to supply the estate. The well, the reservoir and the water tower were thus made obsolete. In 1888/9, the lower part of the tower was adapted as a dwelling for one of the river staff. The well has been capped off now and a house built round the original structures, appropriately called The Wells.

Next door, the Water Tower is currently owned by Geoffrey and June Bone who were most kind in showing me around, as they told me of the history of their most unusual residence. Thanks to their hard work, and no little imagination, it has been adapted into a most comfortable home. It retains the original stone spiral stairs enclosed in a circular tower that is attached to the main building and gives access to each floor. The old tank room is now a bedroom with superb views to be gained from its high vantage point.

The 'Walk' originally ran to the west, but now runs just to the east of the Tower in a north/south direction and is well worth a visit. May you enjoy learning about this part of our history as much as I did.

Retracing our steps to Bush Hill, we soon come across the imposing entrance into Bush Hill Park Golf Course, which many of us will readily associate with Old Park.

The Club started, however, in 1895 on a course to the west of the present one with the clubhouse in Queen Anne's Gardens. With this land being sold for development, they were forced to vacate by Christmas 1911 and they then leased 108 acres of the Old Park estate, laid out as a golf course to Harry Vardon's design, with a clubhouse nearby. It was not until 1920 that the Mansion was leased and used as the headquarters, following a fire at the clubhouse.

The Old Park estate was originally the Home Park of the Manor of Enfield, and Enfield's shopping precinct of today is built on the site of the original Manor House and grounds, which became known as 'The Palace'. Much of the Manor House was demolished in 1792 but part of it survived into modern times until, in 1928, it fell to make way for the extension to Pearson's store.

The house now used as the headquarters of Bush Hill Park Golf Club is thought to be on the site of a ranger's lodge, built on the estate centuries ago. It lay in the centre of a 2,000 year old hill fort, evidence of which can still be seen today.

I must not elaborate too much on Enfield matters, neither shall I delve too deeply into Old Park, as there has been a detailed study and book devoted to the subject in recent years, written by Douglas Haigh, to which reference can be readily made. However, it would be remiss of me to omit the more recent history of this beautiful area and the clubhouse itself, which is well inside the Winchmore Hill borders.

In the early 1800's, the Rev. T. Winchester Lewis settled in Palmers Green and became very friendly with the Taylor and Walker families. He married Elizabeth Walker, daughter of Isaac, who took a lease in her name on part of the Old Park estate including the house itself, an early 18th century building. Sadly, the Reverend died at the age of 33, leaving his widow to look after the estate and their only child, Elizabeth.

The daughter, Elizabeth, duly married Edward Ford who became a very well-known and influential man in Enfield affairs, serving as a magistrate for over 30 years. In 1873, together with the Rev. George Hodson, Edward was co-author of 'The History of Enfield'.

On Edward's death in 1893, his elder son John Walker Ford took over. A northern wing had already been added in 1838 and, in 1875, the distinctive clock tower was removed from Bush Hill Park and re-erected at Old Park, where it still stands today above the roof of the shop of the Club's professional, George Low. With a family of 10 children, J.W. Ford needed more space and, in 1894, the eastern front was extended in the style of the original building.

Like his father, J.W. Ford also served as a magistrate and wrote a book about Bush Hill Park. One of his great interests was the collection of antiques and objets d'art. However, he ran into serious financial difficulties and sold all the 'Contents of the Mansion' in a great sale spread over 4 days in November, 1909. The Recorder's headline 'A Local Treasure House' was no exaggeration. The catalogue listed 1,300 items and ran to more than 70 pages. It included extremely valuable paintings, sculpture, silverware, pottery, china, furniture, books, wines and a wide variety of curios. After the sale, J.W. Ford and his family moved away, yet the house and the estate remained the property of the Ford family until 1920. From 1912, the grounds were leased by Bush Hill Park Golf Club.

Today, over half of the original Old Park estate remains a green and open vista. Two golf clubs (Enfield and Bush Hill Park) and two sports grounds still delight the eye. Much of the remainder has been absorbed by the railway and the development of Grange Park.

Near the extreme north-eastern border of our district stood a superb estate with a lovely house, originally called Bush Hill Park which, in its latter years, came to be known as Clock House. This most imposing mansion was situated at the extreme northern end of Bush Hill, by the banks of the New River. Ringmer Place today indicates its position more exactly.

The house was built in 1685 to the order of Sir Jeremy Sambrooke, with landscape designs by Le Notre, gardener to Louis XIV, and the park eventually covered some 700 acres much of which, you will appreciate, lay outside our region. At one time, it was the home of John Gore, a promoter of the South Sea Company. Then the estate passed to his associate, Joseph Mellish, and later to William Mellish, who died in 1838. Squire William Mellish was an eminent city merchant and a man of high standing. He was a director of the Bank of England for nearly 50 years, a Member of Parliament, a Magistrate and Chairman of the Royal Exchange.

The extensive grounds included several lakes studded with small islands. These stood in ground to the north of the house, between Park Avenue and Private Road of today. The New River, which

The water tower in Quakers Walk, now converted into a private residence, was never used for its original purpose.

Old Park, now the clubhouse and headquarters of the Bush Hill Park Golf club.

An old print of Bush Hill Park, built in 1685, once the home of the Mellish family.
It was later known as Clock House.

flowed by the house, was gracefully increased to three times its normal width, with tapered banks at either end and a boathouse nearby. An engraving dated 1700 shows its true grandeur, with a large stable block surmounted by a clock tower and weather vane.

After Squire Mellish's death in 1838, it remained in private hands until the 1870's, when it was purchased by a land development company. Roads were laid out and building work commenced. As already mentioned, the old clock tower was removed to be re-erected at Old Park, where it still stands today. Parts of the racing and domestic stables were demolished, as were the two great gate pillars and surmounting stone balls. It was the beginning of the end and the final demise of Clock House (originally Bush Hill Park) came in 1927.

The mansion and its country park, once of such grandeur and beauty, had slipped away unnoticed into oblivion. Bush Hill Park now exists in name only as an attractive area nestling between Enfield, Winchmore Hill and Edmonton. It is as well, I think, that we reflect on its history.

Just to the north of this area, we can witness and appreciate the effective shortening of the course of the New River, by the elimination of a huge loop that wound its way to the west of Enfield.

We can still admire the beauty of the river in Southbury Road; by the Civic Centre; in the grounds south of Parsonage Lane; by Gentlemans Row; under Church Street into the Town Park and the Golf Course; – but these sections are all part of a now discontinued loop. This was made possible sometime before 1926, when 3 lines of underground pipe were laid between Southbury Road (near the junction with Ladysmith Road) and Bush Hill (near the end of Walnut Grove). Sometime afterwards, part of the old course was filled in (in particular behind the back gardens of Whitethorn Gardens and by Amwell Close).

Some local residents may remember that, on the night of 15th October 1940, these pipes were badly damaged in an air raid, causing severe flooding. It was a crisis that could have affected London's water supply. At 5 a.m. the next day, 2,000 men of the Pioneer Corps were at work, digging out the filled-in sections of the New River, so that the discarded loop could be revived to fulfil its original purpose. The underground pipes were subsequently repaired by the Metropolitan Water Board when the normal supply was restored and the reopened sections of the old course were filled in again.

Rumours were rife at the time that the damage to the pipes was caused by sabotage and not by German bombs. To keep the enemy in the dark, information was often withheld on such matters but, in this case, the secrecy only fostered more rumour. It is worthwhile exploring by taking the footpath from Bush Hill leading into Amwell Close, where the old river course can be clearly identified.

There has been much discussion on water in this chapter, dominated by Sir Hugh Myddelton and his great project, the building of the New River nearly 400 years ago. We have explored some of the houses that once stood in such beautiful surroundings in this picturesque corner of our region and we have filled our lungs with the fresh air of 'Old Park'. Let us continue our journey.

# CHAPTER 8

## FIRS LANE AND AROUND

IN THIS CHAPTER I should like to look at the south-eastern corner of our region. It may be helpful to look at the map. I refer to the area bounded by Green Lanes in the west and Ridge Avenue in the north. The borders of the N21 district confine us elsewhere. It is an interesting corner that I got to know very well during my boyhood years for my home (83, Farm Road) was in its midst.

Through the centre of this region, on a very approximate north/ south line, runs Firs Lane, with many twists and turns in its path, before it eventually links up the end of Barrowell Green in the south, with Green Lanes in the north. Hence my heading for this chapter.

Further south, in the N13 district, Firs Lane continues as far as Hedge Lane, but I have already written about this very interesting section in my book on Palmers Green.

Let us start in the south and have a look at Barrowell Green, one of the old roads in the district. What is the origin of the name? The word barrow was in common use years ago, meaning a burial mound, so this is a possibility. There has been much research on this question, to which I have added, without reaching any definite conclusions.

There *was* a mound and there *was* a well in olden times. They were situated opposite the modern refuse centre (I should say Civic Amenity Site) of today, on the south side of the road where there once stood a farm. This was later to become Heath's Nurseries. A tiny blind lane, some 50 yards long with a running rivulet in the ditch alongside, led down by the farm and terminated with a pond of bright clear water. This was commonly used as a 'dipping well'. A close-boarded fence ran behind it. This could have marked the boundary but, more probably, was protection for the well.

Doctor John Cresswell has captured the scene in one of his sketches. Just to one side of the well was a large, grass-covered mound with, it is said, a yew tree growing from it. The general consensus seems to be that this was not a burial ground, and the mound has long since disappeared. Its origins remain open to conjecture.

Some of the old documents refer to Barrow's Well and this leads one to the more probable theory that a man called Barrow once owned the farm and, indeed, the well referred to. The actual 'green' appears to have been rather small and situated opposite the farm, in front of where the swimming baths were eventually located.

The old maps show that, a hundred years ago, this whole area was completely open countryside. From Green Lanes, as we crossed the bridge over the New River, there was Hope Cottage on the north side, tight to the river, with spacious gardens front and back. This was the home of Tom Jolly and his wife who cultivated the land and sold fruit and vegetables to the locals. Then, apart from a couple of tiny isolated dwellings, there was nothing until we reached Heath's Nurseries, already mentioned, and The Firs which lay on the north side, where the road still bends abruptly.

As a young boy, Henry William Heath FRHS used to help his father, a nurseryman of high esteem, and would travel up to Covent Garden market with him in pony and trap. The whole family were engaged in the business and it became their way of life. Henry lived for many years at The Laurels* whilst, at various times, other sons and daughters and their offspring operated from:— Heath's Nurseries in Barrowell Green (Arthur); Chequers Green in Palmers Green (at Chequers Keep and The Elms); Firs Lane (Stanley at Myrtle Cottage); Bury Street; and at High Elms Nurseries at Thornwood, near Epping (where Henry died in 1947).

The Firs in Barrowell Green should not be confused with the family residence of the same name owned by the Lake family, which was situated in Firs Lane, and which I have discussed in some detail in my book on Palmers Green. That mansion was demolished about 1820.

The Firs in Barrowell Green will be remembered by many of my readers. It was thought to have been built originally as a private residence, around 1765, but it developed into a farm. The estate, assessed at 25 acres in 1800, was owned by the Clowes family for centuries and was let out to a succession of tenants, some of whom caught my interest.

One was a Mr. Morrison, who had previously emigrated to Australia and was among those who first discovered gold there in 1851. His fortune was short-lived for, before he could return to England, he was robbed by his partners of all the gold he had collected. On his return he had an idea prompted, it is said, by the hours spent in panning gravel and sand in his search for the precious metal. He decided to grow potatoes and cleanse them, using a similar method. He commenced the sale of washed potatoes in Covent Garden and made a second fortune. Mr. Morrison

*The fine old house still stands in Barrowell Green, just west of the junction with Ash Grove, and now operates as 'The Laurels Clinic'.

personally built many of the farm buildings attached to The Firs and planted out the orchard.

Another interesting tenant, though I know little of her work, was Adeline Kingscote who was a great traveller, linguist and prolific novelist. Her pen name was Lucas Cleeve and she wrote most of her books between 1895 and 1907. She died in Switzerland in 1908. Yet another tenant was Mrs. Montague English, daughter of Mr. Wade of Beaumont Lodge, who gave his name to Wades Hill.

In the late 1930's, it became clear that The Firs' days were numbered. The development of the area was gathering pace and the need for road widening at the eastern end of Barrowell Green was becoming a matter of some urgency. The rural scene was being further eroded. The Palmers Green Gazette of May 1937 published some delightful sketches of the old farmhouse, drawn by the local artist Rutherford, clearly showing the old bell. This was mounted high on the chimney stack and was used to call the farmhands to their midday meal. The bell's original purpose may have been to act as a warning or alarm in case of emergency. This was quite usual, centuries ago, when houses stood in isolation and communication was difficult. Written on the boundary wall were the words 'Carter Page – The Firs Nursery'.

The estate was purchased by Southgate Borough Council in 1935, but the sale was subject to Carter Page's lease as a nursery, which still had some 13 or 14 years to run before it could become public open space.

I had a chum who used to live in Barrowell Green and I remember so clearly my visits to his home after school. We would take the footpath in Highfield Road (between Nos. 34 & 36) and come out near the corner shop that still trades today, just a few yards from his family home.

To those of my generation, the name Barrowell Green conjures up a mental picture of the old dust destructor (opened in 1909, rebuilt in 1935) that stood where the modern housing estate has recently been built and, more vividly, the open air Swimming Baths where we spent many happy hours.

The building of the Baths was prompted by the great controversy that arose in 1911. Bathing in the lakes at Broomfield Park had long been enjoyed by the public. Broomfield Park Swimming Club, whose headquarters were there, had become a reputable club with the highest standards. The Borough's Medical Officer for Health, Dr. Ransome, became concerned with the pollution in the lakes and his tests showed that the waters feeding into them were a risk to public health. The order, which was served by the Council, banning all bathing at Broomfield, provoked a tremendous outcry.

The columns of our local Gazette at the time were full of readers' letters, denouncing the action as high-handed and unnecessary. The Swimming Club protested to no avail. It caused much heated discussion in the Council Chamber, but the decision stood. The Council had acted in good faith and they reacted to public opinion, by making the construction of a new open air pool in Barrowell Green a priority. The opening took place on 14th August 1913.

Swimming was a very popular pastime in my youth. We would buy the one penny pink tickets from school which gave us reduced admission to the baths. I can still visualise the queue that would form outside the entrance turnstile, as we waited impatiently to get in. Between the outer gates and the ticket office was an attractive little garden with a curved pathway, where we would wait. I can see us all now, laughing and joking with our rolled up towels and bathing costumes under our arms. I can still see and hear the shrill voice of Mrs. Barrie as she let us in, a little lady with a lot of heart who would not tolerate rowdy behaviour.

There would be a mad dash to the changing cubicles before we did our racing dives (or belly flops!) off the side at the deep end, inwardly shivering at the shock of being immersed in cold water. Then, after a few token widths of frantic activity, we would emerge, stretch our towels out on the raised paved areas around the pool and lay in the sun to dry. Perhaps we would admire the skills of the gymnasts, the sun worshippers, all rippling muscles with bodies tanned to deep mahogany, as they performed on the parallel bars. Otherwise, we could gaze in awe at the graceful skills of the highboard divers, as they plunged like arrows into the deep.

I remember the steaming mugs of Bovril and those enormous halfpenny biscuits we could buy at the shop and, above all, the company and the precious friendships we shared.

It was a very sorry sight to behold in 1983, when I wandered around a demolished pool and surveyed a scene of desolation. Everything had been flattened and a large crater was the only indication of what once had been the pool. The row of majestic poplars had still refused to yield, but they, too, were under sentence. The shrieks of delight from happy children, as they plunged into the pool, had given way to an eerie silence.

The new refuse centre soon took shape on the site of the old swimming baths and next door, where the dust destructor had been, a new estate grew to completion. Somehow, Barrowell Green would never seem the same again . . .

There is a stretch of Firs Lane to the north of Barrowell Green, about 350 yards long, that is quite unique. Right through my boyhood and the wartime years, it remained a quiet country lane. It was one of the last vestiges of countryside to survive in our midst, and it was most reluctant to change or yield to urbanisation.

It was a narrow, winding, tree-lined lane with no pavements, but there were ditches either side and, beyond the trees and hedgerows, lay the open countryside. The trees would make a canopy of green overhead in the summer and we could have been a thousand miles away from any town or city. For us young boys, it was an ideal 'cops and robbers' playground, as we could hide so easily and spring out on the 'enemy'. I particularly remember the hollow tree where you could squeeze inside the trunk and remain invisible for ever.

Today's scene has changed completely, though the land on either side remains undeveloped. On the western side where there was once farmland, nurseries and wartime allotments, there are now green fields and sports facilities. In the distance, built at the top of Laburnum Grove, we can see the 'new' school.

To the east, today, is the Firs Farm complex of playing fields. The area once formed just part of the huge acreage of Firs Farm, the farmhouse being situated in what is the N13 area today, just north of The Fairway. The farm is thought to have been built about 1720 on the instructions of Mrs. Childs, who came from a notable local family (the Childs family were related by marriage to the renowned Udalls of Winchmore Hill). The land was, at one time, the property of the Dean and Chapter of St. Paul's (later the Ecclesiastical Commissioners), who owned 664 acres in the parish of Edmonton, as it was then. It was later purchased from the Commissioners by the Local Council.

The farmhouse was a tall building with a mansard roof and dormer windows, and it had an extensive acreage, extending to the north and east. When it was demolished in 1927, part of the land was later used for housing development and the remainder was converted into sports grounds. My apologies for repetition of a small section from my Palmers Green book but Firs Farm is a case in point where both regions have relevance. In today's terms, although the farmhouse stood in N13, much of its land extended into N21 and mention should, therefore, be made in these pages.

Those Firs Farm playing fields will be remembered by many of us as the site of an anti-aircraft battery during the war. Later on a prisoner-of-war camp took over the area. The family home was just round the corner and, during the raids, I can vividly recall the battery commander's awesome shout of – FIRE! – followed by a tremendous thump that seemed to shake the ground. His commands carried through the night air quite clearly, so at least we were ready for the thump. As school children, we would often collect the shrapnel in the roads, once daylight came. It was a miracle there were not more injuries caused by these viciously sharp and jagged pieces of metal that fell from the skies, though danger seldom registered with our adolescent minds.

We approach the roundabout where Farm Road, Laburnum Grove and two arms of Firs Lane meet. Laburnum Grove is a comparatively new road, created when the development of the area was going ahead in the early thirties. Our family home, 83 Farm Road, was built in 1933 when my parents moved in from Harringay (Umfreville Road). Dad had always wanted a large garden and he was prepared to pay the extra £50 and stretch the mortgage to the asking price, around £900 freehold. I was 4 years old at the time.

Before the houses were built, our home had long been the site of an isolated, black weather-boarded cottage, which faced north and was known locally as Pickerings Cottage. Mrs. Pickering lived here at one time and took in washing. A well-tended front garden was bounded by a hedge, immediately outside which was a ditch. Between the ditch and the rough track that served as a road, was a wide grass verge on which two or three goats were usually tethered. Opposite was a large pond bordered by willow trees, known locally as Tadpole Pond. In wet weather, and at the right season, one would have difficulty avoiding the frogs when walking along the lane at dusk. The land at the rear of the pond was taken up with nurseries and many greenhouses.

Mr. J.W. Bone painted a delightful water colour of the scene, though I have only seen the black and white reproduction in the Gazette of 1935. It all looks so peaceful with the hens foraging along the grassy banks, and a shepherd with his dog guiding some sheep along the rough track that was once Farm Road. There are no pavements or lighting. It is a completely rural scene with only the cottage in view, surrounded by trees and countryside. With the passing of but a few years, we were to witness a total transformation.

How well I remember Laburnum Grove and everyone who lived there. Our family home faced on to Farm Road, but we had a large side and rear garden, stretching around the corner. I can just remember Dad planting the conifer trees, slender specimens no more than 3 feet high. Today (March 1989), they dominate the back

Barrowell Green Swimming Baths will evoke many dear memories.

Firs Lane was reluctant to change despite the pressures of modern development.

155

Pickerings' Cottage which preceded my family home, 83 Farm Road.
This picture was taken in 1926.

Winchmore School in Highfield Road, where we were taught to do 'times-tables'
and 'joined-up writing'.

garden, being about 35 to 40 feet high and of immense girth. Dad had the brick boundary wall built in Laburnum Grove, which is still there today. I remember the high degree of efflorescence that marred its appearance for some years afterwards as the salts crystallized on the surface.

At the end were the gates that led into our garage driveway. These became our 'goal'. Laburnum Grove was the ideal football training ground for me and my chums. I knew every bump, every slope, every drain and manhole cover and all the front gardens, for the ball was apt to go astray sometimes. I remember making a save and, in so doing, getting my fingers painfully trapped between the gates, thus losing two finger nails.

At the top of the road, where Winchmore School is now built, was just a wooden fence with an opening, giving entry to a large area of allotments. It was wartime and we were all being urged to 'Dig for Victory'. Dad had two plots and, being young and keen, I became his helpmate digging them over. It was hard work in the early years, for there was a lot of 'twitch' in the soil which had to be eradicated, not to mention the wireworms. The entry track from Laburnum Grove led on to the allotment shop, or shed as it was more accurately called. It was situated in the centre of the vast area under cultivation and there, a most obliging and conscientious Mr. Ludlow* would dispense seeds and fertilizers to the allotment holders.

Dad had very little spare time to maintain the allotments. His building business was just off the Walworth Road in Southwark and, apart from fire-watching duties, he was on call night and day during the raids, should the area suffer bomb damage. He had a squad of men who were prepared to turn out at a moment's notice in any emergency. As many of you will remember, they were turbulent times, but somehow we coped.

Highfield Road was known as Highfield Row and, at the turn of the century, was still a very quiet backwater. Approaching from the Green Lanes, we would go past The Cedars, (now called Cedar House) to which I have referred in Chapter 6, and over the hump-backed bridge spanning the New River. The road bridge is very narrow and traffic, these days, is allowed to cross only in one

*Mr. and Mrs. William Ludlow were well-known in public life. He was a Southgate Borough Councillor for 6½ years, a prominent committee member and chairman of the Winchmore Hill Residents' Association, and a most enthusiastic and hard-working member, secretary and chairman of the Southgate & District Horticultural Society, before his death in December, 1952.

direction, i.e. towards the Green Lanes. There is, however, a quite separate footbridge on its northern side for the safety of pedestrians. Once over, we can see a charming row of old cottages on our left. These must have been built between 1867 and 1897, as they are shown on the second edition of O.S., but not on the first.

One of these cottages, number 7, has some interesting stories to tell. At ground floor level, to the left of the entrance door, there is a boarded-up opening. This once gave access to the stables and a laundry, which were housed in buildings in the rear garden. The laundry, known as the Highfield Model Hand Laundry, was started in 1860 by Mrs. Woodcock at number 25 Highfield Road and continued in their new home when the family moved into number 7, after the row of cottages had been built. Louise, Mrs. Woodcock's daughter, still lives there and she was kind enough to invite me in to listen to her reminiscences.

She took me through into the garden, and showed me the stables and the attached laundry block. The top storey has now been removed and the remainder is showing the effects of age and Hitler's bombs, but one can still appreciate the original use and purpose of the buildings. Louise remembers Mr. Bassett and Mr. Armstrong, who lived up the road at numbers 7 and 8 Brendon Villas. They were in business as travelling grocers, and kept their horses stabled here until, with the passing of time, they could invest in motor vehicles. How well I remember an ever-cheerful Mr. Armstrong, with his bright yellow van, making his deliveries around the district, when I was a lad. Through schoolboy friendships with their children, my brother and I knew both families very well.

After his wife's death in 1926, Mr. Woodcock tried his hand at frying fish and chips for the locals, but illness and other factors curtailed this enterprise. Coincidentally, there is now a fish and chip shop opposite on the corner with Cedars Road. In my youth this used to be a cafe or 'dining rooms' as they were known then. Louise has seen so many changes during her lifetime. Now retired, she is a trained teacher of the pianoforte and, at one time in post war years, she bred rabbits for show and still retains an expert knowledge on the various breeds. I am most grateful to her, and to my friend Jean Hodge (nee Armstrong), for their co-operation.

Before these cottages were built, a clear stream, in which watercress grew, ran in an easterly direction in a ditch along the north side of Highfield Row. The verge along by the stream was a carpet of wild flowers in the spring. There was a tall signpost, marking the presence of the old Orange Tree Inn opposite.

The old Highfield Row was a very irregular track, wide and spacious in parts, but narrowly confined in others, with curious little nooks and corners. It mattered not a hundred years ago. It was a quiet sleepy quarter with, perhaps, just an occasional haycart trundling through on its way between the farms.

I have a photograph of the old Orange Tree. It was set well back from the line of the adjacent buildings. It was a quaint, two-storey, weather-boarded building. One tiny bay projected at the left hand end of the premises, with a lantern illuminating the adjoining doorway. A single dormer peeped out from the roof. There are no signs of any pavements or public lighting.

Next door but one, there was a tiny little beer house known as The Moulders Arms. It stood well in front of the Orange Tree, severely restricting the carriageway and eventually had to be demolished, to allow more access. It was no more than a black-tarred, wooden cottage where firkins (small barrels) were mounted on shelves behind the bar and the beer drawn off to customers' requirements. The licensee was Mr. Hunt, a brick moulder by trade, hence the name of his premises.

It shows how popular ale and beer was a hundred years ago, when such a quiet, remote area as Highfield Row could support two licensed premises. It was the drink of the masses, on economic grounds alone, and it is no wonder that the brewers skills brought them such rich return, the length and breadth of the country.

The old Orange Tree was demolished in 1912, to be replaced by a fine new public house. The building has been suitably maintained and has endured well, with its attractive green-tiled lower fronts still in good condition. High up on the gables, beautifully sculptured and decorated, are the original pictorial orange tree panels. The brewers, once Christie & Co. of Hoddesdon, are now, appropriately, Taylor Walker.

The familiar yellow stock-brick building of Winchmore School in Highfield Road looks as good as when it was built 75 years ago. Will we be able to say the same about our modern buildings? I have vivid and clear memories of my schooldays there, which I attended from September 1933 until July 1940, i.e. from the age of 4½ to 11 years old. They are mostly happy ones.

I have this vague recall of my mother walking me round on my first day at school and the feeling of fear and isolation, that most of us experience when we are left 'on our own' for the first time in life. There she was, waving goodbye to me from the pavement, and I was alone. I can close my eyes now and see the classrooms, the central corridor, the cloakrooms and the headmistress's study. I can remember, as though it were yesterday, being taught for the first time how to do 'joined-up writing', and all the 'times-tables' up to 12.

Miss Peryer was our Headmistress. She wore glasses, was slightly lame and walked with a stick. Compared with the rest of the teachers, she seemed very strict and keen on discipline, but that was her job and we all respected her. The members of staff under her were a fine team. There was Miss Prince, Miss Boyce, Miss Maynard, Mrs. Hemmings and Mr. Alders. I have happy memories of each and every one of them. Mr. Alders always took the top class, Class 1 as it was called. That was the classroom at the extreme left hand end, at the rear, on the ground floor. He was a grand chap.

Now and again we would encounter the staff from the Senior School upstairs. Mr. Ling and Mr. Bligh made a big impression on me. Mr. Bligh seemed indestructible. He cycled everywhere, often in shorts and, years after I had left school, I would meet him, looking just the same as always. He never seemed to change.

I remember the red tin hut next to the school. In the early 1890's, an appeal was made to the Rev. A.C. Drought, then the vicar of St. Paul's, that a more local house of worship was needed on the eastern side of the parish and, as a result, he built the corrugated iron chapel in Highfield Road. Later on, as a 'new' Winchmore Hill grew up in the Green Lanes, the demand grew for another church to become established in the area. The Rev. A.J. Dewdney, the Rev. Drought's successor, recognised the problem and it was largely due to his efforts that the Holy Trinity Church was built and dedicated in 1908. The old chapel in Highfield Road remained. It was always known as the red tin hut and was used for all kinds of social events as well as church activities. I was much too young to be involved with them, but I do remember my elder brother and some of his friends meeting there.

I can also remember the clinic and the lady school dentist. I can see here quite clearly now, the waiting room and the surgery where we used to go when the toothache got too bad. I remember having gas for the first time, and the sound of the drill – and the pain! Regrettably, these are not happy memories, for the equipment and the techniques were not then as they are today. Dentistry has come a long way since those days.

My last year at Winchmore was clouded by the outbreak of war, announced with appropriate solemnity by Neville Chamberlain. I recall all the preparations that were hurriedly put in hand to combat the menace that was to come. Shelters were built, sandbags filled, gas masks issued and the blackout enforced. For a while, we began to wonder if it was all really necessary. Nothing much seemed to be happening. It proved to be the lull before the storm that was soon to break.

Whilst we are thinking of such matters, I am reminded of an incident much later in the war when, on 24th June 1944, a doodlebug (flying bomb) landed in Carpenter Gardens, near the junction with Highfield Road. It was night-time and we were not in the shelter. My brother and I were lying in bed, when I became aware of a terrible din outside, rapidly building up into a crescendo. It was a loud pulsating, throbbing noise that sounded like a motor bike without a silencer, running at full throttle and emitting umpteen decibels. I rushed to the window to see this terrible object hurtling through the sky ablaze. It was just above the rooftops. I yelled out to my brother and dived under the bed as the bomb exploded.

Most flying bombs cut their engines at high altitude, when we would wait transfixed in the eerie silence as they dived earthwards to explode on impact with whatever lay in their paths. There were a few doodlebugs, however, that hit their targets with the engine still running. This was one such heinous example.

It was a time of great sadness. Amongst the many tragedies, two young sisters suffered terrible injuries and lost both their parents that night. It is as well that we remember the horrors of war.

What more is there to say about Highfield Road? Nearly opposite the school, at the turn of the road, was the entrance to the old gravel pits, next to the row of red brick council houses built in 1899, but of sweeter memory were the two shops, Davies' and Gandy's. Davies' (previously Marriage's) was opposite the Orange Tree. Oh, the delights of the shop with all those glass jars on the shelves filled with brightly coloured confections of every flavour imaginable! What a marvellous new world it was!

My favourite came to be 'Blackjack', a wrapped halfpenny bar at least 10 inches long and $\frac{3}{4}'' \times \frac{1}{2}''$ in cross section. It was a chewy black liquorice toffee and the first bite had the saliva glands working overtime and the taste buds in ecstasy. Then there were the butter toffees, a whole two ounces at a time, and the liquorice pipes. I always saved the bowl of the pipe until last, especially the bit covered with all the red 'hundred and thousands'. The 'chewing tobacco' made us seem very grown-up, even though it was merely strands of coconut covered with cocoa powder. Always popular were the sherbert dabs, those little cylindrical packets covered in yellow wrapping with a hollow liquorice 'straw'. My favourite chocolate bar was Fry's Tiffin – biscuit and raisins covered with milk chocolate. I know many of my readers will have had their own special favourites. Maybe these few reminders will have helped you recall them.

There was a boot repair shop next door. I can still see the cobbler's face, and recapture the ever-present smell of leather and shoe polish. In later years, the premises fell empty and there were long raking shores up the front of the building. No doubt the bomb damage nearby had taken its toll. It is now demolished and the site is empty.

No reference to Highfield Road would be complete without mention of Gandy's. The shop is still there at the end of Cedars Road, tight to the little bridge over the New River, but it now carries the imposing title of Dracox House. What would Mr. Gandy have thought? His real name was James Ganderson and he and his daughter Millie, a very sweet and kind lady, ran the tiny old-fashioned shop that sold everything.

I can see him now, sitting on a stool in the candlelight behind the counter, wearing his cap and grey warehouseman's coat, puffing at his pipe, with a faint smile on his lips. I never saw him without his cap on. There were times when he would be cross and terse with us youngsters, but Millie would always be the calming influence. There were sacks, of rice and sugar I suppose, with a scoop for ladling on to his scales, and the shop had that indefinable sweet aroma of an old-fashioned grocers.

I peered through the windows of, what is now, a flooring contractor's premises. The counter had been pulled out and there were rolls of carpet on the floor, yet I could still see Mr. Gandy sitting there, with his cap on of course.

We must take a very brief look at Farm Road, the very name giving us the clue to its origins and emphasising, yet again, what a great farming area this was. The farm is marked on some maps as Fords Grove Farm (not to be confused with Fords Grove Cottage that became Mortiboys Farm) but, through the centuries, it was known to the locals by the name of the farmer and his family who worked the land. Hence, one sees references to Williams' Farm in Williams' Lane and Jordan's Farm in Jordan's Lane.

The entrance to the farm was on the south side of Farm Road, about 80 yards from the New River, i.e. about opposite where the first house, number 6, exists today. You went along an unmade access road that, beyond the farmhouse, led through to Highfield Road. Well after the turn of the century, Farm Road remained a quiet tree-lined lane with a profusion of wild flowers growing along the verges.

The farmland extended to the south and east and also to the west, on the other side of the New River, across where Queens Avenue is today and right through to the Green Lanes. Here, the boundary was marked with a simple open paled fence. Such was the scene right up to and beyond the turn of the century, before the development of the Broadway.

'There is nothing new in this world' and 'History repeats itself'. These may be cliches, but they are none the less true.

I have been reading about the disastrous gale that swept across our part of the country, uprooting trees and causing severe widespread damage. No, I am not referring to the hurricane, still of vivid memory, on that fateful night in October 1987. Instead, I am referring to the happening on the night of 28th-29th March 1916 and the scene of devastation that unfolded on the following morning. The largest tree to succumb in our area was a massive Cedar of Lebanon on the west side of the New River that fell, forming a bridge across to the Winchmore Hill Cricket Ground on the other side.

The elms, however, were the greatest casualties. Several fell in Station Road, breaking down the iron railings and boundary wall of St. Paul's Institute and completely blocking the road. Several great elms in the garden of the Skinners' Almshouses at Palmers Green (bottom of Fox Lane) were blown across Green Lanes, breaking down the overhead power lines, blocking all traffic and bringing the tramcars to a standstill. Mortiboys Lane (Fords Grove) was particularly badly hit. Here, no fewer than 22 fine old elms were completely uprooted. It was a sorry sight.

Before Mortiboy came to Fords Grove, the old maps show it quite clearly as Middle Lane, i.e. a continuation of Middle Lane (Station Road) on the west side of Green Lanes. At the turn of the century it was no more than a country track. It led over the hump-backed bridge across the New River, eastwards towards the Hyde footpath and onwards into Church Street. It was a path much trod, through the ages, by the villagers of Southgate and Winchmore Hill.

For centuries, until their own churches had become established, the Parish Church of All Saints in Church Street, Edmonton was the religious centre. The local inhabitants would join up in their walk along the footpath through the woods (now Broad Walk) out on to Winchmore Hill Green, then down Middle Lane (Station Road) and across a very leafy Green Lanes. Before the coming of motorised transport, it was common practice for people of all ages and from all spheres of life, to walk for miles in all weathers and think nothing of it.

The journey would continue down what is Fords Grove today, and out onto the Hyde footpath (Firs Park Avenue) cutting through an area rich in nurseries and greenhouses. This apart, the vista was one of open countryside. We were soon into Church Street, going past the cemetery on our right and the cricket ground on our left. Ahead was All Saints and the village of Lower Edmonton.

Another popular walk would take us from Wades Hill down Vicars Moor Lane, briefly into Green Lanes, continuing into the northernmost part of Firs Lane. In 1900, this section of Firs Lane was still known as Vicars Moor Lane. Again, we were in glorious countryside as we crossed the New River and swung east into Jews Corner Lane (today called Ridge Road). Jews Corner, itself, was situated where the Ridge Road of today joins Church Street. The origin of its name is uncertain and remains shrouded in mystery. We have travelled roughly parallel, but to the north of our previous route, arriving once more in Church Street.

On our walk down Fords Grove in those days, the only sign of habitation would have been Fords Grove Cottage, which is thought to have dated from around 1525. This was situated on the south side of the lane where numbers 14, 16, 18 and 20 Fords Grove exist today. Further investigation is both rewarding and worthwhile.

Before we arrived at the cottage, just to the west, some wooden outbuildings fronted the lane but the cottage was set well back, with a very pretty, long front garden bordered by a picket fence. We could go through the gate and down the pathway which led us to a door, centrally placed. The garden was a feast of colour in the summertime and we looked on to a charming, creeper-covered cottage that was the home of Captain and Mrs. Tills. In his retirement, the Captain could often be seen leaning over the garden gate, watching the world go by. Miss Cresswell described him 'as a sweet-faced little old sailor man with a fresh colour and silver hair and whiskers' and Mrs. Tills, 'a tall pleasant old lady, who might have stepped out of a picture'.

Before becoming a Merchant Seaman, Captain Tills had served in the Royal Navy where, as a Lieutenant at the age of 20, he fought at the Battle of Trafalgar. By nature he was a lively, jovial character but his life was shattered by the tragic loss of his only son Frank who, at the age of 27, lost his life at the siege of Delhi in 1857, at the time of the Indian Mutiny*. Under the great walnut tree in the garden, he built a cairn of stones which, from the descriptions sent to him, resembled his son's grave in India. He would sit by his shrine and meditate for hours. It was a loss that he never came to terms with.

Captain Tills, his wife and his invalid daughter, Ellen, died in quick succession between 1864 and 1866, leaving the remaining daughter, Charlotte, in the old cottage to face the world alone. Charlotte's artistic talents had long been apparent. Mrs. Todd of Uplands (widow of David Todd, an eminent surgeon, who had died in 1839) had previously arranged for Miss Tills to attend the Royal Female School of Art in Queens Square, where she showed great promise. Now, on her own, Charlotte struck out and obtained employment in town, drawing and designing. It meant a journey by horsebus for her every day, nearly 2 hours each way, at a cost of half a crown return fare. It was a brave decision for a young girl to seek her independence in this way in the 1860's.

Mary Savill became her live-in maid at Fords Grove Cottage and continued in this capacity after 1871, when Miss Tills moved to the low white house on the Green (now the site of La Fondue) where she ran a school. Henrietta Cresswell was one of her pupils, both at Fords Grove Cottage and at the Green. Mary Savill remained in service until Miss Tills' death and was bequeathed all her effects. She eventually sold the Captain's Trafalgar Medal to a collector, together with the Indian Mutiny Medal that had been posthumously awarded to Frank Tills.

After Charlotte's move to the Green in 1871, Fords Grove Cottage became the home of the Mortiboy family. Mortiboy, a noted cowman, farmed the surrounding land over a wide area. The lane became Mortiboys Lane and, for the last 40 years of its active life, the old cottage became known as Mortiboy's Farm. It was in urgent need of repair. Just think, it had stood there even before the arrival of the New River (1609-1613), looking out over a completely rural scene. So much has changed. Let us be thankful that the houses in Fords Grove are still allowed an open aspect with a few hedges and trees, and a chestnut fence bordering a well-tended sports ground.

The old cottage's original horn window panes had long since given way to leaded glass but the roof and floors were in such bad

*We are reminded of Lieut. General John Campbell of the Royal Engineers and his wife Henrietta, who lived in Chase Road, Southgate. Their heroism at Gwalior, 200 miles south of Delhi, at the time of the Indian Mutiny has been referred to in 'Southgate – A Glimpse into the Past'.

condition that, in 1911, a Closing Order was served by the District Council, deeming it to be unfit for human habitation. It remained defiant until its demolition in 1923, by which time it had been totally enveloped in ivy and other creepers. Fords Grove Cottage was no more.

We should be grateful for the open space east of the New River, stretching from Fords Grove across to Firs Lane, that we know today as the Paulin Ground. To trace the origin of its name and, indeed, to explore many facets of Winchmore Hill's history, we need to concentrate on the task in hand.

I have already touched on the history of Winchmore Hill Cricket Club in Chapter 6, where I discussed the mansion of Fords Grove, its grounds and the Busk family who lived there. The Busks remained the landlords of the Club at Fords Grove for the first 40 years since its inception in 1880. The ground occupied their private park, on the Firs Lane side of the ground, and iron hurdles on wheels were rolled into place to prevent the cattle straying onto the pitch.

We must now move on to the Mann and Paulin connections with the Club, both very wealthy families forming an integral part of the popular brewers Mann, Crossman & Paulin. The Paulins, incidentally, were of Huguenot extraction, their ancestors having fled from Southern France in the late 17th century and settled originally in Berwick.

The story becomes a little complicated here. There was inter-marriage between the families and some of the christian names repeat through different generations. Moreover, there are a number of different homes involved. In my quest for clarity, I have kept my account as straightforward as possible but it has not always been easy. Please bear with me.

The Club, set up at Fords Grove in 1880, was originally called the Winchmore Hill Village Cricket Club. Nine years earlier, in 1871, the Winchmore Hill Cricket & Lawn Tennis Club had been established at Roseneath by Thomas Mann. It was a rather high-class gentlemen and ladies club, with the cricket and tennis being played in the beautiful grounds of the founder's estate. Thomas Mann was the President, and the Secretary was our old friend, Thomas Teshmaker Busk of Fords Grove.

Roseneath House was situated on the south side of Vicars Moor Lane, between the railway and Ringwood Way, and the estate of 14 acres stretched as far south as Middle Lane (Station Road) and

The old Orange Tree in a quiet and sleepy Highfield Road.

The new Orange Tree, built in 1912, retains its classic style and elegance.

Fords Grove, looking east. The Paulin Ground is on the left
opposite the wooden buildings.

Fords Grove was no more than a country lane. This picture is taken from the
junction with Firs Lane, looking due west towards the New River.

east to Radcliffe Road. Ringwood Way and Radcliffe Road are comparatively new roads, and are only quoted to help us realise the extent and position of the grounds. It is generally recognised that the cricket table, the wicket itself, was very adjacent to where Winchmore Hill Bowling Club have their green today, near the 'elbow' of Radcliffe Road.

Thomas Mann and family had come to live in our area in 1858, initially at Laurel Lodge in Church Hill, before Roseneath was purchased in 1867. His son Sir Edward, who was created a baronet in 1905, continued to live at Roseneath until his move to Norfolk in 1913. In 1914, William Thomas Paulin, who had married Thomas Mann's daughter Fanny, presented Roseneath to the War Office, fully equipped as a voluntary hospital for wounded soldiers. By October 1915, the number of beds had been increased from 40 to 50 and, in total, more than 1,600 soldiers passed through the hospital.

May I go off at a tangent at this point to mention Sir Edward's third son, Francis Thomas Mann, who became a legend in the cricketing world? A mighty hitter, he succeeded 'Plum' Warner as captain of Middlesex in the 1920's. In 1921, he brought to Fords Grove the first MCC side to play the Club. This was the same season that 'F.T.' led Middlesex to win the Championship and in the following season, 1922-3, he captained England in all 5 Tests against South Africa. In turn, his son, Francis George Mann, born 1917, successfully captained Middlesex and England after the Second World War. I saw a lot of cricket in those days. Middlesex had a brilliant side in this, the Compton-Edrich era, and 'F.G.' played a significant part in welding it into a team. F.G. Mann, D.S.O., M.C. was President of Winchmore Hill C.C. from 1961 to 1970.

I must return now to the Paulin family and another home. I refer to Thomas Paulin, father of William Thomas (already mentioned) for it was Thomas who, with his family, moved out from Stoke Newington in 1865 and came to live at Beaulieu, where they stayed for 8 years. His son, William Thomas (1848-1931), would have been 17 at the time. I have described Beaulieu and its history in more detail in Chapter 6.

It was in 1877 that William Thomas Paulin married Thomas Mann's daughter, Fanny, at Christ Church Southgate, having previously acquired the Broadfields estate of 14 acres between Wades Hill, Church Hill and Houndsden Road. They farmed the land and kept a fine herd of Jersey cows. In family tradition, William maintained a close interest and support for the London

Hospital and, in 1893, became a local J.P. He and his family were true friends of the village, helping out in numerous ways and for a variety of causes. They were especially supportive of St. Paul's in Church Hill. There were two daughters, Ina and Irene. Already a Vice President of Winchmore Hill Cricket Club, William Paulin became President in 1895 on the death of Thomas Teshmaker Busk, and he held this office until his death in 1931.

His wife, Fanny Paulin, died in 1901 at the early age of 49 years. She played a significant part in establishing the great rapport that existed between the family and the village. She was known as the 'Lady Bountiful' of Winchmore Hill, due to her many good deeds. Her obituary included 'the poor had no kinder friend than she and many have lost a generous and sympathetic benefactor'.

It was in her memory, in 1903, that her husband erected St. Paul's Institute in Station Road. It served many needs during its lifetime of over 50 years. Now demolished, the site has been redeveloped as a District Sorting Office for the GPO. The foundation stone was salvaged and was placed by the west door of St. Paul's in Church Hill. It can still be seen there today. It simply says:-

To the Glory of God
and in Memory of Fanny Paulin
This Building was erected by
William Thomas Paulin
Ina Dewdney
Irene Paulin
1903

Arthur J.B. Dewdney
Vicar

In July 1902 at St. Paul's Church, Miss Ina Paulin, eldest daughter of William, and the Vicar, the Rev. A.J.B. Dewdney, were married by the Bishop of London. Alongside the church the bride's father had Vicarage House built, still used by the incumbents to this day. Regrettably, because of illness, the Vicar was obliged to resign in 1907 and, on the advice of his doctors, emigrated to Canada with his wife and baby daughter. The younger daughter, Irene, remained unmarried and was a great help to her father in running the estate and looking after many of his local interests.

After the 1914-18 war, the Busk family's Fords Grove estate was put up for sale. It comprised about 75 acres with frontage on to Green Lanes, including the land occupied today by Ridge Road (once Jews Corner Lane), Halstead Road and Firs Park Avenue. It was divided into 9 lots, Lot No. 2 of 20½ acres being the Paulin Ground as we know it today. At the sale in 1920, Mr. W.T. Paulin's successful bid of £8,000 for Lot No. 2 was to prove of tremendous and lasting benefit to the Cricket Club and the community as a whole. He set the rent at 2½ per cent of the purchase price, to stand for the next 40 years, and vested the freehold with his daughter Irene.

In the New Year's Honours List of 1929, it was announced that the Club President had been knighted for services to the London Hospital, where he had been a Life Governor for over 50 years but, two years later, Sir William died. Winchmore Hill had lost a true friend and a great benefactor.

It was in the September of this year, 1931, that both the Broadfields and the Roseneath estates were put up for auction by Mr. E.J. Westoby, our local estate agent of renown, and it marked another step from village life towards suburbia.

Generous of spirit, Miss Irene Paulin was intent on continuing her father's policies. Initially, she leased the ground to its various users but, in 1929, she granted a new 5 year lease of the ground to the Cricket Club at an annual rent of £200. This embraced the whole of the 20½ acres.

In succession to her father, Miss Irene accepted the Presidency of the Club and, in 1932, agreed to the provision of 3 hard tennis courts. The following year (1933), she permitted Sunday play from 2 p.m. for the first time in the Club's history. And so her generosity and goodwill continued and was extended through the war-time years. As leases expired, they were renewed on terms greatly to the benefit and advantage of Winchmore Hill Cricket Club. In 1948, she graciously accepted the proposal that the Ground should, henceforth, be known as The Paulin Ground, in grateful recognition of the great services rendered by her and her ancestors.

Miss Irene Paulin died on 30th June 1960. In the terms of her Will she granted the Club a 99 year lease, to be dated from the 25th December after her death, at an annual rent of one shilling.

There have been many great families who have given our area invaluable service, and done incalculable good through the centuries with their generosity, their wisdom, their energy and their goodwill. None more so than the Paulins.

I hope I have conveyed the facts clearly and accurately. The essence of the story goes well beyond the mere setting up of a cricket club. It has a far deeper meaning and was of much greater consequence over a wide spectrum of life, the effects of which can still be appreciated today. I realise that I have strayed occasionally beyond the limits indicated in my chapter heading but, hopefully, you will appreciate the reasons.

We finish the chapter with a last look at Firs Lane. Travelling northwards, 100 years ago, we would have passed a large grassed triangle at the junction of Firs Lane and Jews Corner Lane (Ridge Road). It was commonplace to see a few gypsy caravans resting here awhile, for there were wide grass verges on which their horses, ponies, and sometimes goats, could graze. The edge of the sports ground was lined with hedges and, in the ditch alongside, a stream of clear water ran continuously. Just at the top of the hill was the New River, where a bucket could be lowered to be filled with the 'sweet waters of Hertfordshire'.

Percy Road did not exist then but, at the junction just behind the triangle of green was Woods Cottage, once a tiny picturesque dwelling, finally vacated in 1931 and demolished soon afterwards, for it had become dilapidated. Firs Lane now swings abruptly in a north-westerly direction. With the Paulin Ground on our left, we climb the hill and go over the New River bridge.

Immediately on our right was the site of Riverbank, a lovely house set in 6 acres of grounds extending either side of the River. It had started life, about 1760, as a modest sized cottage and was known then as Butts Farm. Over the years, it had been enlarged into an imposing residence of character and was renamed Riverbank. There was a large yard, stabling, coach-house and a spacious lawn leading down to a most attractive stretch of the River. Other parts of the grounds were adorned with some fine specimen trees including maidenhair, Judas, cypress, chestnut, horse chestnut, walnut, a few tall elms and a far-spreading cedar. There was an orchard with 60 fruit trees and an abundance of flowering shrubs.

Mr. Bresano, born in Nice and commonly known as 'The Frenchman' lived there, with his wife, at the end of the last century. He and Madame Bresano were very proud of their home and grounds, which they kept in perfect order. He was a manufacturer of artificial flowers, with a factory in the City. An expert in his field, he introduced new methods of production, hitherto unknown in this country.

How pleasing to be able to report that the old name Riverbank has been retained in the development of the houses and flats which, together with the Exchange, are built around the four sides of a pleasant open green between the New River and Green Lanes.

An so we emerge into the main road, with the Firs Banqueting Suite on our left and the Telephone Exchange on our right. I hope you have enjoyed our meanderings along Firs Lane and Around, and have followed the somewhat indirect route I was obliged to take. This south-eastern corner of our region contributes a great deal towards the fascinating story of Winchmore Hill.

# CHAPTER 9

## FOND MEMORIES

I DECIDED that the title of my last chapter should form the basis for the title of my book for they are, indeed, fond memories. Throughout these pages, here and there, I have included some personal recollections which I hope have proved stimulating.

Being a local boy, I thought it would be in order to put the book to bed with a few more of these observations. They are not of any great moment or importance, yet I understand, from your letters, that they often provide the key to a hidden store of fond memories from your own experience in life. It is for this reason, alone, that I include my final meander down Memory Lane. I hope I am successful in unlocking the door and energising those dormant brain cells.

When Cresswell, Willis, Regnart, Mason and Newby were writing, I am sure they were inspired by this fact. They realised they were living through a period of great change and, before it was too late, they wanted to record their own situation and that of the past. They could foresee that future generations would be growing up in an entirely different environment. The old scenes and characters could, so easily, 'fly forgotten as a dream' and slip forever from our view.

That way of thinking is very applicable and pertinent today for, right now, the changes around us are no less rapid or dramatic, if only we could realise it.

I was very flattered when Mathew, a 13-year-old schoolboy, came to see me recently, asking advice on writing a book and doing the necessary research into local history. 'How should I go about it?' he enquired. I helped him all I could. Did he have a camera and was he capable of taking photographs? It appeared that this was one of his interests. 'Right' I replied, 'I suggest you go around the locality now, taking pictures and making notes of what you see for, by the time you grow up, it will be an entirely different scene.'

Indeed, many of the photographs I took, even 5 years ago, are already historic in the sense that they already represent the past. As this young lad grows into manhood, there will be so many changes along the way. When a new history comes to be written in 2039, or whenever, he will have today's background and scenes on which to base his story. I hope I have made my point clear.

Our memories are a strange phenomenon. They provide us with a kaleidoscope of many images, each one inconsequential and unimportant but, taken in their entirety, a pattern does emerge. We are looking at a picture, piece by piece. As with a jigsaw, each piece conveys little but, when we put the pieces together, the whole becomes meaningful.

I can see the milkman with his horsedrawn float, and the baker with his pushcart, making their deliveries up Laburnum Grove. We had one neighbour, keen on gardening, who always hoped the horse would perform its natural functions. He was seldom disappointed. He would immediately appear with his pail and shovel commenting, 'very good for the rhubarb'. Today's electrically propelled vehicles would vex him greatly.

Around our locality, when I was young, there were three ice cream companies vying for trade with their delivery tricycles during the summer months. They would ring their bell to attract attention and, in no time at all, children would gather round as the salesman delved into his ice box to bring forth the goodies.

Walls were the favourite with their familiar dark blue tricycles and 'Stop Me & Buy One' signs. The 'Snofrute' was the most popular with us, not only because of its price (one penny), but because it was a most refreshing water ice with a delicious fruity flavour and crumbly texture. It was triangular in section and came in a light card sleeve, printed in blue and white chequered squares. The vanilla bricks cost twopence (old currency) and were individually wrapped, with wafers one penny a packet. The vendors of Eldorado and Dairy Ice Cream offered keen competition. The last named was considered to be the creamiest of the three, slightly more expensive, and sold in a little cardboard carton.

Ice cream remains very popular today and is sold in a much wider variety of flavours and textures. 'Soft' ice cream, dispensed from special machines, has become increasingly popular in recent years. The much-loved trike has been replaced by a van, with its amplified jingle, making an occasional visit to satisfy a reduced demand. Most households possess freezers today, so the ice cream can be bought in bulk at the supermarkets and stored until required.

Davies' sweet shop in Highfield Road, in effect, served as the school tuckshop in my youth, for it was only about 75 yards up the road from the school gates.

I have never been a great lover of chewing gum. Once the flavour goes, what have you left? However, several of my chums enjoyed the habit, and would buy their packets of 'Beech Nut' in Davies' shop or from the machine on the wall outside. These were the small packets containing 4 or 5 white-coated pieces of spearmint flavoured gum, not the brown strips you see today. The machine was just a metal box, painted yellow, with blue lettering indicating where to insert your halfpenny and where to turn the knob to receive your packet. It also advertised the fact that, for every fourth halfpenny inserted, you received an extra packet free. It was, obviously, a game of chance inviting you to spend, in the hope that there had been three unlucky customers before you.

One classmate, who shall be nameless, had filed a notch on the knob and discovered that, when this pointed to one o'clock, the bonus was due. He shared his secret with a few of his friends. We could only have been about 9 or 10 years old at the time. I found myself glancing quickly at the knob, each time I went along. It never showed at one o'clock and I began to despair.

The great day arrived at last. I could not believe my eyes, but there was no mistaking – the scratch was pointing in the right direction. There was no one around. With trembling hands I put my halfpenny in and turned the knob. There were my two packets, waiting to be picked up. My feelings were a mixture of elation and guilt (mostly elation!). It was like getting something for nothing. I collected my reward and hurried away. I never did it again because my conscience kept pricking me and, in any case, I never did like gum! Unimportant and inconsequential? Yes, but why then do I remember every little detail?

People often ask what my generation did for entertainment as we grew up, through childhood, into our teenage years. Just how did we spend our time? What were our interests, and how did we amuse ourselves during those formative years?

This was the age before the arrival of television or videos. It was an age when the pubs were frequented more by our parents and the older members of society, whereas today they cater more for the younger generation, and serve as their social centre. We were just kids at school and, give or take a year or two, had barely reached double figures, when the war came in September 1939.

The cinema was our great source of entertainment. I have written in all my books about the picture houses of Southgate, Palmers Green and Winchmore Hill. I must be careful to avoid repetition but, from my humble reflections, I hope you will have gathered and can appreciate the affection with which they were held. My feelings are shared by the many thousands who became regular cinemagoers, both before and during the war. If you mention the Capitol Winchmore Hill, the Odeon Southgate, the Palmadium and Queens Palmers Green, and the Ritz Bowes Road to my generation, then the eyes will light up in fond recognition.

'Let's go to the pictures', we would say and the pulse quickened immediately. When the 'A' film was on, we could always ask a grown-up to 'take us in'. There was no harm done. We had escaped into another world. It was always best to go with somebody – our parents, our school chums or our girl friend, and talk about it on the way home. That added to the enjoyment! Many a courtship, it is said, started in the cinema, where the amorous pursuits on screen may have been surpassed by those in the back row of the stalls.

As soon as we reached our mid-teens, the other great social activity was ballroom dancing. It was extremely popular. Many attended dancing classes to learn the basic steps of the waltz, quickstep and foxtrot and, if we were very brave, the tango and the rumba might be attempted. The records of Victor Sylvester and his Orchestra were usually on the turntable as we practised over and over again. We bought books of tuition, with all those strange diagrams showing the positions of one's feet, the right always shaded black and the left in white, with separate instructions for the ladies and gentlemen to follow. One could easily get tangled up and finish in a heap on the floor.

Joking aside, ballroom dancing is a lovely, graceful way of giving expression to some beautiful music in the arms of your partner. What more could you want? You do not have to be an expert, just a few basic steps will suffice.

Many of us met our ultimate partners in life at a dance, my wife and I included. We first met at St. Paul's Institute in Station Road, a very popular venue in our youth. There would be a dance on there every Saturday evening, and sometimes in mid-week too. I remember it so clearly and the bands that played there under the control of their respective maestros, Billy Lawrence, Harry Crystall and Joe Hart.

I would arrange to meet my chums outside the dance hall. The refrains of soft music wafted across the cool evening air, inviting us in. There was a sense of eager anticipation as we bounded up the stone steps to hand in our tickets. As we opened the inner doors, the music became louder and we could see a few couples progressing around the floor. The band was on stage, with the familiar mellow tone of Harry's violen doing full justice to the tune. They were playing a waltz.

We always liked to start with a waltz for, provided you kept to the '1,2,3 together', you could not go far wrong (famous last words!).

We looked around quickly. There was a whole line of attractive, shy young girls sitting it out, looking so pretty and demure in their best dresses. Were there any that we knew and, if so, could we pluck up courage to ask them for a dance? If the truth be known, we were more shy than they were.

Sometimes the Master of Ceremonies would have a job to get people on the floor and, to 'break the ice', the band would play a Paul Jones. The boys formed an inner circle, going one way, with the girls outside, facing them, going the other way. When the music stopped, you introduced yourself to your nearest partner and started to dance. Many a romance started that way.

There would be the interval when soft drinks, sandwiches and cakes would be served. The lads would get together and talk about the girls they had danced with. We would 'compare notes' and then ask 'Yes, but are you taking her home?' If so, this was taken to mean you had really enjoyed one another's company and, maybe, would like to meet up again. The band would return and the dancing continued, usually until about 11.30 p.m., when the waltz 'Who's Taking You Home Tonight?' signified the end of proceedings, and a most enjoyable evening.

In the course of writing this book, I was delighted to make contact and meet up with Harry Crystall, now 73 years young, and still living in the Bounds Green area. He remembers with affection the post war years, right through to the late fifties, when he played regularly at St. Paul's Institute. Harry is semi-retired and still very active, though his dance band days are long since over. 'When rock and roll came in, I moved over' he says, 'but I still love the old tunes.'

The dance music of that era included many beautiful melodies, and the music lives on. Ballroom dancing has not died, but its popularity with the young, as a social pastime, is a thing of the past. Who knows, one day it may return.

I can remember back to pre-war days, when I was still a small boy in short trousers. Mum would sometimes take us for a 'ride in the country', as she described it. We usually went with a neighbour and her son, a playmate of mine. The two Mums led the way, each clutching a carrier bag containing our picnic. We straggled behind, usually kicking a ball about or playing catches. Having walked up Station Road, we caught the train heading north. Our destination was Crews Hill, Bayford or Cuffley, the latter always being my favourite. The whistle blew and the train reluctantly stirred into action.

The neat houses of suburbia soon gave way to green fields and, just a few stops later, the train screeched to a halt, and it was time for adventure. The memories of those days all blur into one, but I can still remember the thrill and adventure of the train ride itself, warm summer afternoons, walks down country lanes, and sitting in the shade of a tree having a picnic tea. This unfailingly consisted of tomato and cucumber sandwiches so, if I should ever wish to recall those days, I can always make myself another sandwich or, alternatively, board the train at Winchmore Hill station, heading north.

As I grew up, one of the great joys of my boyhood, along with many of my contemporaries, was to go on cycle rides. We had quiet roads then, almost devoid of traffic and, if there were any dangers, we had the innocence of youth, and did not know about them. I would go cycling with my school chums to a variety of destinations, but I remembered those train rides with Mum and would often say – 'Let's go to Cuffley!'

From my home, it was up Farm Road and over the bridge. In the early days, there were grunts and groans as we tackled the hill, up off the saddles, determined not to dismount. My first 26 inch wheel Raleigh arrived one Christmas, complete with Sturmey Archer 3-speed gear to make life easier. What luxury! On past the Capitol we would go, along Green Lanes to Masons Corner and into Green Dragon Lane. Another climb to the top, and we were turning right, past the hospital, and descending Worlds End Lane. With a few twists and turns, we were soon on The Ridgeway, in glorious open country, and on our way to Botany Bay, where we swung into East Lodge Lane. The delights of Cuffley lay ahead, where we could have a bottle of Tizer and a bar of Crunchie. Sheer ecstasy!

During those early excursions into Cuffley, I had been made aware of the 'war memorial', set in a quiet secluded grove near The Plough inn. I vaguely knew it was something to do with the First World War. As I grew up, I still had an affection for the place, and I continued to go there. I was older now and saw things with a different pair of eyes. I went back to the war memorial and read the inscriptions. It seemed that fate had drawn me there. I wanted to know more about it. Just who was William Leefe Robinson, and what were the events that led to the building of this monument, all those years ago? This led me to a wealth of most enjoyable research into the exploits of this very brave young man, who shot down the first German airship over British soil. But that is another story.

What other amusements were there? There was snooker at the

Palmers Green Billiards & Social Club, to which Dad took me at an early age, where I met many of his friends. It was more of a minority sport in those days but, through the medium of television, how popular it has become. This will continue, for it is a marvellous pastime providing, as it does, so many different situations. One can play a thousand games and each one will be entirely different. There is little risk of boredom and the skill factor is high.

I was taken many times to see the master, the great Joe Davis, who dominated the game for several decades prior to his death in 1978, at the age of 77. Joe won the world snooker title every year from its inception in 1927 until 1946 (there was no competition 1941-45). After the 1946 final, Joe retired from world championship play, though he continued with exhibition matches. Throughout his career, he always played with the same cue, one he had bought second-hand for seven shillings and sixpence when he was 17 years old.

Many of our sports and pastimes enjoy but a transient popularity. They bask for a while in glory, then fade from the scene as quickly as they entered. Sometimes they can be rekindled. One sport on the crest of a wave just after the war was ice hockey, which attracted very good crowds to Harringay Stadium to see the needle matches between Harringay Racers and the Brighton Tigers. The sport lives on, but with more limited appeal these days.

Through my boyhood and teenage years, family visits to the West End theatres were rare. I suppose it was the age we lived through, the wartime, the difficulty of travel, and the expense. After the war, we had the opportunity to see some of the great American musicals that were staged in London.

There was always the local Intimate Theatre, where you could be assured of a first-rate production, week in, week out. It was founded in 1935 by the late John Clements, who set and maintained the highest of standards. He appeared in no fewer than 200 plays, most of which he directed. Though he left in 1940, the theatre continued to be a very successful training ground for many in the acting profession. Richard Attenborough made his very first appearance on stage there in the summer of 1941. Sadly, it closed in January 1988.

One entertainment, almost extinct now, is the local music hall or variety theatre. We had two within fairly easy reach, the Wood Green Empire and the Finsbury Park Empire, both long since gone. It was a great treat to go to either, just to see a 'live' show. I can remember many of the turns, some famous, some not so, including

The familiar Wall's ice cream tricycle which invited us to 'Stop Me and Buy One'.

Crusty loaves filled the baker's cart on his daily deliveries.

181

*(left)*
The late Sir John Clements, who founded the Intimate Theatre in 1935. His stage and film careers reached the very highest levels.

*(below)*
Built as the Gas Company's Showrooms in 1911, the building was badly damaged by fire in 1988.

182

singers, dancers, comedians, ventriloquists, jugglers, magicians, contortionists, impressionists, etc.

One act I saw at Finsbury Park is etched forever in my mind, a staged table tennis match between Victor Barna and Richard Bergmann, both world champions. The rallies went on and on, and Barna's forehand drive was forcing Bergmann further and further from the table. Eventually, he completely disappeared from view into the wings, though still managing to chop the ball back into play with unerring accuracy. It was awe inspiring in its intensity, with the dark and dashing figure of Barna smashing the little white ball with all his might, only to see it looping back from Bergmann's defensive play. I realise it was part of the act, but I marvelled then, as I do now, at the control and the speed of reaction exercised by the great exponents of the game.

How did we amuse ourselves at home? We could always read or play cards. The popular card game, at the time, was solo whist. I recall us playing this for hours in the air raid shelter during the days of the blitz, when the air raids tended to last a long time.

The favourite board game in my youth was Monopoly. My chums would often come round and play, especially in the school holidays. The game would go on for hours, and we would all become quite animated, buying houses and hotels, and dishing out wads of 'money' as though it was confetti. It gave us a feeling of power, I suppose. My aim was to buy Trafalgar Square, Fleet Street and the Strand, if I possibly could. They seemed to be my 'lucky' properties, along with the Water Works. Others were more ambitious and plumped for Park Lane and Mayfair.

We had some great times with Monopoly, an ideal game in many ways, for it keeps the mind fully stretched and it teaches you how to lose, which I did quite regularly! It is still played today, but there have since been many other board games devised, many of them equally entertaining and enlightening. Monopoly, however, was one of the first.

We had a small size snooker table that could be placed on top of our dining table. Problems arose trying to cue near the cushions, for the walls and furniture got in the way. Dad compromised by shortening one of the cues. It was not ideal, but it taught me the rudiments of both snooker and billiards.

The dartboard, too, had pride of place in the dining room. In those days, the News of the World sponsored a team of players, who travelled the circuit of clubs, playing exhibition matches. We occasionally saw them at the Palmers Green club. Jim Pike was the leading exponent in those days. He would go 'round the clock' in doubles, with a sheet of newspaper covering the board. His wife would stand sideways on, close to the board, with a cigarette between her lips and Jim would proceed to knock the ash off with his first dart. There were no failures. I often saw Jim Pike, for he lived close to our business premises in Walworth, and opened a shop in Kennington. Darts is another game that has won great popularity, following its coverage on television.

How different are the rewards today for the sporting giants. Joe Davis and Jim Pike never amassed a fortune. Eddie Hapgood, a very great fullback who captained Arsenal and England for years in the thirties, had a maximum wage of £8 per week during the playing season and £6 in the summer. There are countless similar examples. Their lasting reward was reaching the top of the profession and playing to the peak of their ability, for club and country. They could not do more. Some of them, in later life, may have ruefully counted the cost and made comparisons, but there could be no regrets.

I must not forget the wireless, the greatest home entertainment of all. There was a whole host of regular weekly programmes and artists that became household names. A snatch of the signature tune is usually enough to release a whole flood of memories.

Those I recall vividly are:- In Town Tonight (the opening, together with the Knightsbridge March, was a masterpiece in itself); Music Hall; Monday Night at Seven (produced by Ronnie Waldman with Puzzle Corner); Band Waggon (Richard Murdoch and Arthur Askey); Itma (Tommy Handley); Garrison Theatre (Jack Warner); Sincerely Yours (Vera Lynn); Hi Gang (Ben Lyon and Bebe Daniels); Happidrome (We Three); Music While You Work; Much Binding in the Marsh (Richard Murdoch and Kenneth Horne); Workers Playtime (direct from the Works Canteen); The Brains Trust (Dr. Joad, Commander Campbell and Julian Huxley); and the dance bands of the day such as Ambrose, Jack Payne, Geraldo and Henry Hall, not forgetting the American influence of Glen Miller with his 'new' sound and swinging arrangements.

Later on, other programmes became popular such as:— Mrs. Dale's Diary; Have a Go (Wilfred Pickles); Round the Horne (Kenneth Horne); Take It From Here (Jimmy Edwards, Dick Bentley and June Whitfield); The Goon Show, etc. etc.

I have listed them as they have come to mind, not in any special order. I could expound on each and every one of them, but that is not the objective. What I hope it *has* done is to awaken some of *your* memories of these and many other programmes that captivated audiences of millions, before the age of television was fully established.

An outstanding recollection that I have, relates to the world heavyweight title fight, between Tommy Farr and Joe Louis. The broadcast came live from New York and my parents allowed me, as a very special treat, to stay up very late to listen in. I can see us all now, crowding round the console radio we had in the front room, listening to the commentator giving a blow-by-blow account of the great battle going on in the ring, over 15 rounds, between these two great fighters. That night, together with thousands of others all over the United Kingdom, we were willing the young Welshman on to, what would have been, a tremendous upset – victory over the 'Brown Bomber'. It was not to be.

In what must have been a terribly close decision, Joe Louis was given the verdict, and we all felt so sad for the gallant loser. Tommy Farr accepted the decision without rancour and won many hearts that night. It must have made a very deep impression on me for, when I checked the date of the fight, I found it to be 31st August 1937. Then, I was but 8 years old.

Music continues to play a meaningful part in our lives, as it has done through the ages. The world would indeed be a poorer place without it. Today, we hear it on television and radio, on cassette players in our cars, on tape decks and compact discs in our homes, complete with a complicated array of hi-fi equipment. We can even walk along with it plugged into our ears, if we wish.

Years ago, it was the wireless and the gramophone. As a teenager, I would save up my pocket money to spend on the latest '78' in one of the record shops in Palmers Green on Saturday morning. I was not alone. I still have many of my '78's' which I treasure. Bing Crosby, Frank Sinatra, Glen Miller, Perry Como, Dick Haymes, Dinah Shore, Doris Day, Al Jolson, Mario Lanza, and Deanna Durbin are just a few of the artists appearing on the labels. This not only gives some indication of the 'pop' music of my teenage years, but also indicates how strong the American influence was then. I remember the thrill when Dad bought our Ferguson radiogram with the autochange. This meant we could stack 8 records on the turntable and listen to them play, one after another. The extended play records of 33 and 45 r.p.m. had not yet arrived.

One of my great loves, from a very early age, has been sport. This was fostered largely by my father, a keen sportsman himself and a loyal Arsenal supporter from his early childhood. It was well before the war, in 1935, when he took me to Highbury Stadium to see my very first game of professional football. I was 6 years old at the time and I felt so important as we sat in the stand. I was absolutely thrilled. From the very start, my enthusiasm for the game knew no bounds and I implored him to take me again. There was no persuasion needed. 'Up the Gunners' became the cry, and already my allegiance to the lads in red had been forged, that was to last a lifetime.

I was 7 years old and the 1936-37 season was approaching, when Dad gave me one of the best presents I could ever have hoped for – a season ticket at Highbury in a seat next to him. Could life have more to offer? I was overjoyed.

From then on, Dad and I were regular supporters, and the bond between us strengthened. He taught me the finer points of the game, and told me about the great team that had been built up during the Herbert Chapman era (1925-34). Many of that team were still playing under his successor, manager George Allison. The following season, our seats were switched to the new East Stand, Row G nos. 121 and 122. The season tickets cost £3-16s-0d (£3.80).

More than 20 years ago, I wrote my first book. It was called 'My Sporting Heroes'. It will never see the light of day, but it serves to remind me of some of my thoughts at that time. It was dedicated to my father, 'for all his help and encouragement in those early years, which engendered in me the love of sport'.

What a team Arsenal had in those days! They won the League Championship in 1931, 1933, 1934, 1935 and 1938. The reserves won their League no fewer than ten times between 1927 and 1939. Some of the players, like the great Alex James, were nearing the end of their careers, but their successors were to prove equally illustrious. I must be wary, for I have found the key and unlocked the door to so many memories, it is like entering Aladdin's cave. Before I realise it, we shall soon run out of pages.

Dad and I hardly missed a game at Highbury in the ensuing years. We would watch the first team one week, and then the reserves. I got to know every player then, their style of play, their strengths and their weaknesses. I can remember every player I ever saw in an Arsenal shirt very, very clearly. I can quote all the first team and reserve team players, without any reference to books or programmes. If only my more recent memory was as good!

Saturday became a great day for me, which continued well after the match. Tea time on Saturday was, by tradition, fish night and Mum would prepare those delicacies we all loved. It would be kippers or smoked haddock with real butter, grilled herrings, sprats or bloaters, or perhaps shell fish, shrimps or prawns, plus several slices of new crusty bread and butter.

Even today, when kippers are being cooked, I can close my eyes and hark back to those golden days. I see the family sitting round the table at Saturday tea time, holding an inquest on the latest match. The world then seemed such a marvellous, uncomplicated place. There is a lot to be said for the innocence of youth!

Then the war came. Highbury was taken over as an A.R.P. post by the authorities, and White Hart Lane became Arsenal's new home ground which they shared with the host club, Tottenham Hotspur. To avoid long distance travel, regional leagues were formed and competitive soccer continued. Very early on, the government realised it was important to encourage all forms of entertainment, in order to maintain and bolster public morale.

Petrol was severely and strictly rationed and could only be used for essential purposes. This is when Dad and I took to our 'bikes'. White Hart Lane was no distance, but we cycled many a mile, to all the London grounds, to see all the away matches.

This was the time when 'guest' players were allowed. The call-up had left many teams sadly depleted and they were allowed to enlist the help of players from other clubs who may be stationed nearby. Aldershot, for instance, a comparatively small club, were able to field the full England half-back line – one of the advantages of being a military town.

Arsenal, too, fielded several guest players, including a young inside forward from Blackpool, serving with the R.A.F., who captivated everyone by his tremendous speed and acceleration, apart from his goal-scoring abilities. His name was Stanley Mortensen, one of my very special sporting heroes. My mind is filled with such gifted players, and many marvellous matches.

It is strange, too, how the small details stick in the mind, like the refreshment vans and cafes where we would buy a mug of tea and a bacon sandwich; the many back gardens where we left our bikes for threepence, along with hundreds more; the problems of finding them after the match was over; the eager anticipation as we went through the turnstile; the many team changes announced over a sometimes inaudible tannoy. With the hazards of war, the printed programme was never more than an approximate guide as to who was actually playing; the elation, or otherwise, at the end of the match, depending on the result. I don't recall any crowd trouble whatsoever and the banter was usually good humoured. I must confess my visits to professional football matches are very infrequent these days.

My other great love had long been cricket, fostered by an early visit to Lords Cricket Ground to see the great Middlesex County side. Lords is a unique place. You can feel the atmosphere and the history the moment you enter. It is indefinable and yet immortal.

As with football, wartime cricket had to be played on an entirely makeshift basis but, again, there were some great performances and some exciting matches to be seen. Our local clubs and our cricket fans benefited greatly with the formation of two very strong wandering sides, London Counties and the British Empire XI. Packed with international stars, these teams would visit and play against local teams, usually to help the war effort and in aid of charity. I remember some great matches on the Paulin Ground, Winchmore Hill and at many other local clubs such as Southgate, Enfield, Edmonton and Alexandra Park.

I have many sporting heroes but my greatest of all was, and is, Denis Compton, as both footballer and cricketer. I quote the words verbatim that I wrote about him more than 20 years ago:—

On the cricket field his talent shone like a beacon. Though the war cut short his career by slicing six years completely away, who will forget those post-war years, when his marvellous batting was like a breath of spring in the acrid smoke of after battle. When the jaded minds of weary people, so long affected by air raids and the tragedies of war, cried out for some release, some escape from bitter memories, then the sun shone and Compton swept for four at Lords, and the world was a civilised place again.

I hope this sporting interlude has not proved too wearisome. I have only touched on a wealth of reminiscence, most of which does not belong here. My apologies if I have not been sufficiently restrained.

How quickly things are changing today! Another two of our old shops in Palmers Green, Gamble's and Bourlet's, have disappeared and now Wisepart's premises stand empty. There has been massive redevelopment alongside the railway between Aldermans Hill and Broomfield Lane. Some of the fine houses overlooking Broomfield Park have been demolished. The development of the Grange site moves on apace, and what is happening to the old Minchenden School playing fields? The Asda store has opened off Chase Side, and it appears another supermarket may take over the old Bart's ground in Green Lanes, Winchmore Hill.

It all substantiates the point I made in the first few paragraphs of this chapter. I reiterate to all who may be interested in our local

Denis Compton leaves the field at Hastings (September 1947) having passed Tom Hayward's record for a season's aggregate, set in 1906. One of the great players of all time.

history, look about you today and record the scene, for much of it will soon be gone.

Judging from your letters and phone calls, the Directory of Shops I included in my Palmers Green book was extremely popular. I am very pleased, for it achieved its purpose, i.e. it triggered off a host of your own memories. That was the real objective.

As far as Winchmore Hill is concerned, I have included a brief Directory of the Broadway shops as they were in 1939 and then, fifty years on, as they are today in 1989. The shops in other parts of the village, for example around the Green, have been discussed at some length under the appropriate chapters, hence my limitation. I just had to draw the line somewhere!

Many of my boyhood years are clouded by memories of wartime and the hostilities. Clouded is not the right word, for it was not an unhappy period of my life. But it was a time of shortages and hardship, with the severe rationing of food, clothes, sweets, petrol etc. The air raids made a deep and lasting impact on us all, the more so when we knew of families who suffered tragic losses in their wake. Rationing, like National Service, did not finish with the end of hostilities. It continued for many years into peacetime until, gradually, more supplies became available and normal service could be resumed.

The family home was in Farm Road and, therefore, our centre for shopping was the Broadway. Up the road, over the hump-backed bridge across the New River, and we were there. As a boy I frequently ran errands for Mum, taking those all too familiar ration books with me to join the queues and obtain our precious supplies.

I got to know the shops and the shopkeepers quite well, in addition to my fellow shoppers. After all, standing in line awaiting one's turn, it was only natural to pass the time of day with those nearby. It is amazing how well the community spirit prevailed, and how high the morale of the people was then, in spite of all the difficulties.

Mum would never forgive me, if I didn't start with her favourite – Sainsbury's. Most of the more senior residents will recall the much cherished branch of this, now massive, supermarket chain. I remember its cleanliness and its black and white tessellated floor.

The entrance was central, and immediately to our left was the meat counter. I can see the butcher now, and the jolly lady with rosy cheeks and curly hair who would assist him. I never saw her without a smile on her face, which sometimes helped to relieve the depressing sight of what was on offer at the meat counter. I refer to quantity, not quality. If I remember rightly, the bacon counter was further down on the same side. The cash desk was central at the far end, under the clock.

It is a strange phenomenon. My memory tells me that our dear old Sainsbury's was a huge and spacious shop, yet I am sure, if I could re-enter it today, I would feel almost confined and restricted. We have become used to the huge supermarket stores now, and size and space are relative to our experience. Anyway, be it so humble, it was a super shop.

On the right hand side, half-way down, was the butter and margarine counter. It was not pre-packed then, but came in large solid blocks of rich creamy yellow. The counter assistants would take great delight in paring off our two ounces with their wooden spatulas, and beating it into shape with a frenzied attack. I am sure it released all their inhibitions and frustrations. You never saw an unhappy assistant on the butter counter! The little lump of butter or 'marge' would finish up looking quite sorry for itself, but with a nice ribbed finish impressed by the face of the blades, to be finally wrapped in a piece of greaseproof paper.

Talking of food, I should highlight a pre-war memory here before there were any shortages (except money!). I do remember, in the thirties, Mum would, on rare occasions, be very extravagant and provide a great treat for Sunday dinner. This would consist of roast chicken with all the trimmings, plus Libby's peaches and Fussell's cream (tinned) for dessert. This was considered sheer luxury then, only to be afforded at Christmas time, or for some very special celebration. It was such a rare and eagerly awaited treat, that it has become so well remembered.

Today, chicken is a popular dish all the year round, within the means of most, and tinned peaches and cream are scarcely considered a luxury. There are many similar examples, most of which reflect on our modern, cost effective (though sometimes controversial) production methods.

Occasionally the opposite applies. I can recall that, most summers, the bumper plum harvest would cause prices to fall to between twopence and threepence per pound (about 1p in today's currency). We had stewed plums ad infinitum for dessert, and Mum would buy up large quantities for bottling and jam making, to see us through the rest of the year. This was common practice then, certainly amongst our neighbours, but not so today. Plums never seem to be that cheap anymore.

What about the greengrocers? Mum usually went to Burke's. I say usually because, in the wartime, it was often a case of shopping around for what was available. Always obliging and anxious to help their customers Reginald Burke* and his wife were great stalwarts of the Broadway scene. How long and hard they worked! In their latter years, they were assisted by their two sons, Alan and Ivor.

Alan, who sadly died some years ago, took over the Broadway shop and Ivor managed another branch at Masons Corner. Both continued in the family tradition with a cheerful and friendly approach towards all their customers. Though he left the greengrocery trade many years ago, Ivor still lives locally. The Burke family will be remembered by many with affection and gratitude.

Mr. and Mrs. Young were the proprietors of the other greengrocer's shop on the Broadway. They were a young hard-working couple who deserved to do well. The trade was a very arduous one in those days (and probably still is), for it entailed an early morning trip to Covent Garden, long before most of us had left our beds.

Do you remember the chemists? Boots' branch remains at No.751, though the layout of the shop has been completely changed. I well remember the manager there, a kind bespectacled man, who one day helped to remove a piece of grit from my eye. Most chemists are compassionate people. Like doctors, they deal with people in trouble who need their help and guidance.

Some may remember Mr. Walters (now Atkinsons) and John Whitehead, both in this category. The latter served the area for 43 years, before his retirement in 1975. His slight, bearded figure was a permanent feature, it seemed, on the Broadway. The business thrived because of his personal individual attention. There was always a ready smile to accompany his advice, given in that familiar high-pitched, rather squeaky voice.

The shop was a curious mixture, many of the fittings dating back to the Victorian era. Some of the apothecary jars and bottles were very ancient, one jar dating back to 1717. When the shop closed, these were sent to Sotheby's for sale. John Whitehead looked forward to his retirement. After a few months holiday in Italy, he planned a tour of all the cathedrals in England and Wales. I believe he went to live in Brighton.

---

*Reginald's brother Albert founded the Palmers Green shop in 1913, later managed by his son Roy, prior to its closure in 1988. The Winchmore Hill enterprise started around 1917, in a small half shop on the west side of the Broadway, before settling across the road at No.754.

Alfred Brimley's timber yard always looked in a state of chaos, but this was not the case. They held tremendous stocks there of sawn and planed timber, sheet material and a wide variety of mouldings. The foreman had no trouble in locating your requirements. He knew exactly where to lay his hands on that length of old-fashioned moulding, needed to match up to some existing.

Sandell Perkins, by comparison, is extremely orderly, neat and tidy. I must admit I do not get quite the same thrill as I once did, wandering around the racks of the old Brimley set-up, sorting out a nice straight length of 2″ × 1″ or an 8′ × 4′ of ½″ ply. Today I have to ask where the 50mm × 25mm is kept, or have they a 2440mm × 1220mm of 12.5mm ply. Much simpler, I am told. Working with wood is one of life's joys. The smell of an old fashioned joiners' shop evokes vivid and pleasurable memories of my apprenticeship days.

The only other shop we used, on the south side of Compton Road, was the Electricity Board showrooms, where you went to settle your account or buy some light bulbs and fittings. It is now a car showroom.

As we look at the shops listed in 1939, we ask which of them survives today, 50 years on? Boots has already been mentioned. Smith & Sons, builders' merchants, remain and have expanded their premises. In spite of all the supermarket competition, those two familiar butchers shops, Buttery and Bain, still face one another across the Green Lanes. The Midland Bank continues as does Leslie Ricketts, the estate agents. Charles Ledsham, opticians, are still on the Broadway, though they have moved across to the west side.

Last, but by no means least, Wragg Brothers* continues to supply us with good quality menswear with their customary courtesy and friendliness. What service they have given us over the years! The shop was opened by the brothers Cyril and Donald Wragg on 15th July 1933. It was only a half shop then, previously used for secondhand furniture. Regrettably, Cyril died 6 months later, but Donald continued the business, enlarging the premises and soon establishing a name for fine quality goods, served with a kindness and understanding that may be considered old-fashioned today. Many of his staff have endured over the years and, though Donald has retired, several of them remain to maintain and continue the shop's fine reputation.

There are several shops that have changed hands, yet continue in the same trade. I can think of Findlater's off licence, now Oddbins.

*The shop now trades as Wragg's Menswear.

We always had a bottle of their Dry Fly sherry at Christmas time. King's, estate agents, have given way to Adam Kennedy. Read's the paper shop, Yarrow's and Edwards', confectioners, have changed hands but still operate in similar, though somewhat diversified, trades. The same can be said for Maison Woodcraft, now Cutting It Fine.

Haslehurst, the jewellers, became Houghton's on 1st June 1953. We can go back to 1923, however, when Mr. and Mrs. Woodgate, grandparents of Brian Houghton opened their shop in Station Road, Wood Green, having started in Mays Road a year or so earlier. Brian's parents both worked in the Wood Green shop and will be remembered, too, by their Winchmore Hill customers. The Houghton family were highly respected and a much loved part of the Broadway scene. For many years now, Brian and Brenda have maintained the family tradition. As jewellers, one could trust and rely on their judgement. Nothing was too much trouble. They had a wide circle of regular customers, who became accepted as friends. It was a two-way thing. Such relationships in business become less common as the years go by. They recently decided to take their leave of the jewellery trade and are sadly missed, though happily the new owners continue to operate in similar vein.

Penny's are a very popular bakers who trade in the shop once occupied by Westbrook's. Johnson's, the dry cleaners, then a half shop, has become Carlton's. Johnson's was the only dry cleaners who had any success in removing the grass stains from my cricket whites. I remember the lady in there so well.

The half shop adjacent to them was Frank Eastman, gents hairdressers, my regular barbers all through my schoolboy days, though later on in my teens I often patronised the shop in Station Road, near the old Skinners premises. The popular request then was 'short back and sides' and one's hair would be cut regularly once a fortnight. A little Brylcreem provided the final touch, and we emerged with well-defined parting, and hair all sleek and shiny.

How well I remember Frank Eastman's tiny shop. As you entered, you sat on wooden chairs against the right hand wall. You could either watch those being shorn in front of you, or read from a pile of magazines on a table nearby. From their dog-eared condition, Picture Post, Titbits, Lilliput and Men Only appeared to be the most popular. The last two were pocket-size magazines illustrated with photographs then considered very daring and risqué. Page 3 of the tabloids today is probably far more explicit. Many will recall Mr. Eastman. A smart, lively, cheerful man, he always wore a grey tunic buttoned up to the neck.

194

What other shops spring to mind from the old days? The Co-op in Compton Road, Howells the bakers, who also had two branches in Palmers Green and Blake Cooke's, the old fashioned grocers. I can visualise the latter very clearly, and the two gentlemen who served there. The counters were on the left hand side, with the cash desk on the right. Sometimes the service was not all that quick, for much of one's order had to be fetched from the back, where the main stores were situated. Nobody seemed to mind.

In the rear, left hand, corner was a separate busy counter coping with our Post Office requirements. All this has long since disappeared, and a recent visit revealed a nondescript premises standing forlorn and empty. The one reminder of days gone by is the pillar box on the pavement outside.

The shop for fresh fish was MacFisheries. Do you remember the manager? He had dark wavy hair and rather thick black-framed glasses, with quick movements and slight abruptness in his manner. I do not mean that disrespectfully.

I shall always remember the first consignment of whalemeat during the war. There was an acute meat shortage in those days, and advance government publicity was claiming whalemeat to taste just like a prime juicy steak. Mum sent me for some, and I joined the queue at MacFisheries. They were doing a roaring trade, and had been obliged to impose their own form of rationing. We only had it the once. It was reasonably tender, but our palates were not accustomed to its rather oily taste. Some people's reactions were favourable but most, like us, preferred to go without.

Do you remember Mrs. Churchill, who supplied the flowers we needed for those special occasions, and the Evans wool and ladies wear shop? They also had a branch in Harringay. The Wattle, too, springs to mind, and the ladies who served there. Tucked away in cosy corners, we could always enjoy the home made cakes and other fare served in such intimate surroundings. It had such a friendly atmosphere. I remember Salmon's as a hardware shop, where you could buy paraffin, tools in the early DIY days, and a whole host of kitchen utensils. I think it later diversified into a grocers. They had branches in Southgate and Palmers Green.

I have written about the United Dairies shops in my Southgate and Palmers Green books. They were a welcome feature of our suburban areas in this period, usually corner shops where all the fresh milk, cream, butter, cheese and eggs would be dispensed from large refrigerators, which lay behind the counter. The dairy on the corner of Station Road and Green Lanes was typical. With its chequered black and white tiled floor, it was always beautifully cool and spotlessly clean. The lady assistants would be immaculately attired in freshly laundered white coats with matching caps.

At one time, dairy products were considered of vital importance for our good health and well-being. At school, during the war, drinking our daily 1/3 of a pint of milk during morning break was considered as imperative as carrying our gas masks at all times. Today, the medical experts recommend moderation pointing out the dangers of high cholesterol, a word almost unheard of a few decades ago.

With the growth of supermarkets, the dairies have all disappeared now. Most of us shop in bulk, say once a week and, with a refrigerator and a freezer to preserve our perishable items, there is no problem. We should not forget that it is only since the war, and then only gradually, that most homes have been able to acquire their own refrigerator, let alone a freezer. Before these modern times we live in, we had to shop more on a day-to-day basis, and the dairies had an important role to fulfil.

Before Hobbs Wilson took over, the old dairy was empty for a long, long time and it became shabbier and shabbier. I would pass it with more than a pang of regret, knowing how it had looked in its prime – so proud and erect, so clean and well cared for, such an important and integral part of our shops on the Broadway.

Those comments would apply, too, in no small measure, to the old Tottenham & District Gas Company's Showrooms, where my Uncle Harold was manager for many years.

With the development of the Broadway, and the extension of the tramway northwards from Manor House as far as Winchmore Hill in 1907, it was apparent that, before long, there would be further growth in the area. Our street lighting at this time was all powered by gas, and there is an article in 'The Recorder' of October 1910, praising the Tottenham & Edmonton Gas Company* for the high standard of lighting provided along the Broadway and the Palmers Green shopping areas, which had already been developed.

On the home front, too, gas lighting was still in vogue, the 'Bland' lighting being very popular. These were the days of the old ornamental iron brackets, decorative glass shades and the very fragile gas mantles. I realise there are many of us who will have seen and remember the old gaslamps, but there is a whole new generation to whom they are unknown.

*It became the 'Tottenham & District Gas company' in 1928.

It is interesting to note a full page advertisement in 'The Recorder' of January 1911, which states:– 'Electricity will soon be available in Southgate. Residents and shopkeepers should bear this in mind and incur no further expenditure upon present lighting arrangements'. This was the start of keen competition between the gas and electricity authorities, involving not only lighting but, as time went by, heating, cooking and other appliances.

In 1911, the Gas Company's fine new building was completed. It featured a clock, once the Broadway's reliable timepiece, and a very fine decorative turret on the Queens Avenue corner.

Many years later, I was to become well acquainted with the splendid showrooms on the ground floor where the latest cookers, fires, waterheaters etc. would be displayed. H.J. Bartlett, my uncle, became a highly respected figure in Gas Board circles and a very popular man locally. I would occasionally call in to see him, and witness his enthusiasm as he demonstrated the latest cooker.

Some of my readers may remember 'H.J.', not only for his work in the showroom, but also for his fine piano playing. We had a baby grand in our front room and, whenever he called, he would be persuaded to sit down and play – anything from Chopin to the latest hit of the day. I would listen entranced. 'All The Things You Are' by Jerome Kern became a favourite and he never forgot. He was always much in demand, for his musical talents were quite exceptional.

For the last few years of his working life, he was transferred to the Tottenham showrooms. He remained a bachelor, and retired on his 60th birthday. To his great delight, he bought a cottage in a small Suffolk village, where he soon made his mark and became much loved by the villagers. Always a religious man, he became closely involved with the local church, where he played the organ and composed music. Just a year or so later, in 1968, he died of leukaemia.

In recent times, for reasons of economy, the policy has been to close many of the old showrooms and, regrettably, Winchmore Hill was an early casualty. The premises have been occupied by a furniture company for some years but tragedy struck early one morning in 1988, when fire broke out and caused extensive damage. Hopefully, the work required to restore the building to its former glory will not be long delayed.

And so we come to the end of another chapter and the end of this book. May it have given you some pleasure, and rekindled as many fond memories for you, as it has done for me.

# ACKNOWLEDGEMENTS

THIS, MY THIRD BOOK, has taken up countless hours of research and thought, as well as writing. To follow, there has been the work involved on the publishing side, and the liaison and attention to detail with the printers. Then, at long last, the great moment arrives when the book is born. The van arrives and we start unloading. The boxes are stacked high, and the dining room takes on the appearance of a warehouse. Hopefully, the telephone will ring so that distribution can begin. I seem to have been here before, some other time.

Closeted in my study, the hours have fairly melted away, causing many other tasks and duties to be ignored. I am very grateful, yet again, to my wife Sheila for her understanding. She has helped with the long and arduous (but very necessary!) job of reading the manuscript, checking the proofs, making suggestions, correcting grammar and punctuation etc. In short, she has been a tower of strength.

Once again, I would like to thank our Local History Department for their forebearance and their kind assistance with my researches into this project. We are indeed fortunate in this borough to have such a fine team led by a most knowledgeable Graham Dalling, our local history librarian. I thank him for reading the final text and for his help and encouragement throughout.

Church histories tell us a great deal, not only about ecclesiastical matters, but also about much wider aspects of local history. The churches have played a large part in the community life of our area as it has grown from village to suburbia, and we are indebted to those who have recorded the events during the early years of creation.

The local newspapers are a great source of information. They provide a complete and on-going record of every aspect of our social history. Every article and every advertisement adds to the picture, enabling us to visualise and fully appreciate the lifestyle of years gone by. Our thanks are due to the editors and their contributors for recording the scene over a long period. I refer especially to men like Arthur Willis ('Memorabilia') and Tom Mason, but there are many others besides.

We are not overburdened with books on the local history of our region. Indeed, that has encouraged me to try and make good the deficiency. There is the much treasured 'Memories of a Lost Village' by Henrietta Cresswell, 'The Story of Southgate' and 'A Southgate Scrap-Book' by Tom Mason, 'Old Southgate' by Herbert

Newby and 'Memories of Winchmore Hill' by Horace Regnart. Other valuable publications come from 'Walker Round', David Pam, Douglas Haigh, and Denis Hoy.

'Exploring the New River' by Michael Essex-Lopresti is thoroughly recommended whilst 'The Hertford Loop' by Peter Hodge and 'All Stations to Enfield Town' by Graham Dalling will be enjoyed by all railway enthusiasts. 'The History of Winchmore Hill Cricket Club, 1880-1980', compiled by Tony and Jennifer Bath, has been particularly well researched and presented. It reveals a fascinating insight into some of the great families connected with cricket and with village life. Likewise the history of the Bowling Club adds to our knowledge on social history, as well as the game itself.

My list is far from complete and I apologise to those whose names I have not mentioned. I convey thanks to *all* my fellow scribes for their contributions, large or small, for they have helped to widen and deepen our knowledge of local history.

Keith Surtees has a clear and retentive memory of his lifetime in Winchmore Hill, with a fund of knowledge on local characters and events. He kindly agreed to write the foreword and read the final text for me, for which I am very grateful.

There have been many others who have helped me on my way, such as Geoffrey and June Bone with details of the Water Tower in Quakers Walk; Fred Rudling of Winchmore Hill Garage; Louise Woodcock on the Highfield Laundry; Jean Hodge (nee Armstrong); Mrs. Anstee for allowing me to look over the old bakery; Dorothy Adams of the hairdressers in Compton Terrace; Elizabeth Bowen for showing me round the old Downes' premises on the Green; Miss Tewson for her kind hospitality and memories of Broad Walk; the owners of 42 Station Road for showing me 'Cotterstock'; Tony Lewis for his conducted tour of a revitalised Grovelands; Mrs. Lacey, the Secretary and Miss S. Swinburne, ex-Headmistress of Keble School; Dick Simpson for his chats about the old days; Gwen Webb for her stories about the Hemingtons; Dorothy Cole for her memories of The Shrubbery; Donald Wragg, Ivor Burke and Brian Houghton for details of their family businesses. My thanks to all of you and to all those I have omitted to name. Your help is very much appreciated.

A very important part of my research has always been looking at all the old photographs it is possible to trace. One can readily learn so much from them. A page of text, describing the old Green Dragon inn, will not convey the true image half as effectively as a glance at an old photograph. Then, again, it is very often the incidental detail in the photograph which catches our eye, and tells us so much more. I thank all those early exponents of the art, for their foresight in capturing the scenes of yesteryear and for their expertise.

My grateful thanks to the Local History Department for again allowing me access to search their files and borrow some of the old prints to include in my illustrations, also to John Clifford, Murray Woolveridge and Miss Tewson who willingly gave permission for me to use some of their photographs. Once again, I took my Pentax camera around the locality to record the modern scene, using the old FP4 black and white film. It is a very satisfying medium and makes a refreshing change from the more vivid colour slide and print films we usually employ today. Ron Chapman has again assisted with the processing.

Coupled with the early photographers, I should like to thank the early map makers who contribute a great deal to our understanding the changing face of our area through the years. The Ordnance Survey maps, in particular, are a mine of information which, like the photographs, can be referred to time and time again.

Lyn Smith must be used to my rapidly deteriorating handwriting by now. All the arrows, stars, deletions and strange instructions that I cram into the margins, have failed to prevent her doing a first-class job in typing the draft and final manuscripts. Many thanks, Lyn.

Macdermott & Chant, the printers and bookbinders, have again helped me with this volume. I convey thanks to the staff of their St. Albans, Welshpool and Enfield factories for looking after my requirements.

Finally, my grateful thanks are accorded to all my readers for their interest and support for, without them, this book would never have been written.

# DIRECTORY

## THE BROADWAY SHOPS, 1939-89

The shops listed include those in the Broadway, Green Lanes between the Police Station and Station Road on the west side and between either end of Queens Avenue on the east side. I am grateful for the assistance of Kelly's Directories for helping me to compile the 1939 list. I compiled the 1989 list in the July of that year, and have assumed the names marked on the shop fronts to be those under which the company currently trades. There has been some renumbering and 'half' shops have been created or made whole with the passage of time. My apologies for any errors unwittingly made.

| 1939 | No. Green Lanes | 1989 |
|------|------|------|
| **West Side** | | |
| Winchmore Hill Police Station ......... | — | ........ Winchmore Hill Police Station |
| Alfred Brimley, Timber Merchant .... | 699 | .. Sandell Perkins. Timber Merchants |
| Northmet Electricity Board ............. Showrooms | 701 | ............. Bruce Motor Group. Car Showrooms |
| Northmet Electricity Board ............. Showrooms | 703 | ............. Bruce Motor Group. Car Showrooms |
| Fords Grove Motors ..................... | 705 | ............. Bruce Motor Group. Car Showrooms |
| W. Warwick, Florist ..................... | 707 | ............. Shorrock Security Centre |
| Wm. Clark, Cafe ......................... | 709 | ...... Porter Services Electrical goods |
| Wm. Clark, Cafe ......................... | 711 | ...... Porter Services Electrical goods |
| | 713 | ............... Ladbrokes Bookmakers |

### COMPTON ROAD

| | | |
|------|------|------|
| London Co-operative Society, ......... | 715 | ................ Landfield Dry Cleaners |
| Ann, Home-made cakes ................. | 717 | ......... Little Angels, Childrenswear |
| Kathleen Francis, Gowns .............. | 717 | ........... Lauren, Wools & tapestries |
| James Cross, Cabinet maker .......... | 719 | .. Smith & Sons, Builders merchants |
| Smith & Sons, Builders merchants ... | 721 | .. Smith & Sons, Builders merchants |
| Oceana Laundry, Receiving Office ... | 723 | .. Smith & Sons, Builders merchants |
| King & Co. Estate agents .............. | 725 | ........ Adam Kennedy, Estate agents |
| Findlater Mackie Todd, Wines ........ | 727 | ............. Oddbins, Wine merchants |
| Lewis Howell, Baker .................... | 729 | ......................... Brooke Fabrics |
| Hills, China dealers ...................... | 731 | ................... Magnum Travel Co. |
| John Whitehead Chemist ............... | 733 | ......... Savva & Sons Leather goods & shoe repairs |
| John Whitehead Chemist ............... | 733 | .. City & Metropolitan Building Soc. |
| Rupert Alexander, Grocer & P.O. ... | 735 | ...................................... Vacant |
| Charles Read & Son, Stationers ....... | 737 | .... Cherry's, Tobacco & Newsagents |
| MacFisheries, Fishmongers ............ | 739 | .......................... Anna's Bakery |
| F.L. Sewell & Sons, Hosiers ........... | 741 | ............. Odyssey Records & tapes |

201

| | | |
|---|---|---|
| Churchill's, Florists | 743 | Charles Ledsham Opticians |
| J.N. Buttery & Co. Butchers | 747 | J.N. Buttery & Co. Butchers |
| J. Sainsbury, Provisions | 749 | Nanak's Supermarket |
| Boots, Chemists | 751 | Boots Chemists |
| Evans Stores, Hosiers | 753 | Chloe, Ladieswear |
| J. Salmon & Son, Grocers | 755 | Lisa, Kitchens |
| Burtol, Dry Cleaners | 757 | Broadway Fruit Basket |
| Fred Yarrow, Confectioner | 759 | Newsmart, Newsagents & confectioners |
| Wragg Bros., Menswear | 761 | Wragg's Menswear |
| Wragg Bros., Menswear | 763 | Wragg's Menswear |
| United Dairies | 765 | Hobbs Wilson, Kitchens & bathrooms |

## STATION ROAD

**East Side**      QUEENS AVENUE

| | | |
|---|---|---|
| Aladdin, Dry cleaners | 736 | Groves, Travel agents |
| Joshua Steed, Tailor | 738 | Autosure, Insurance agents |
| Charles Edwards, Confectioners | 740 | Jardins, Newsagents & confectioners |
| Eastman & Son, Dry cleaners | 742 | Fairgreen, Estate agents |
| Progressive Boot Repairs | 744 | Brahams T.V. & Video Service |
| John Harries, Draper | 746 | Harpers, Ladies Salon |
| Easiephit Footwear | 748 | Presswarm Windows |
| J.T. Walters, Chemists | 750 | Atkinsons Chemists |
| Mrs. Barnett, Cafe | 752 | Abetone Restaurant |
| Reginald Burke, Greengrocer | 754 | X-It Ladies & Childrens Wear |
| Maison Woodcraft, ladies hairdresser | 756 | Cutting it Fine, Unisex Salon |
| French Cleaning & Dyeing Co. | 758 | Brahams, T.V. & Video |
| Keating & Rumens, Electrical | 760 | Peter Graff Estate Agents |
| Madame Irene, Draper | 762 | Peter Graff Estate Agents |
| L. Fine & Co., Grocers | 764 | Buon Pranzo Restaurant |
| Pauline Marks Childrenswear | 766 | Computer Car Sales & Service |
| Reginald Haslehurst Jewellers | 768 | W. Houghton, Jewellers |
| Harry Westbrook Bakers | 770 | Penny's Bakers |
| Arthur Bain Butchers | 772 | Arthur Bain Butchers |
| Johnson Bros., Dry Cleaners | 774A | Carlton, Dry Cleaners |
| Frank Eastman, Gents hairdressers | 774 | Carlton, Dry Cleaners |
| S. Young, Greengrocers | 776 | T. Craddock, Fruit & greengrocer |
| V. Norman, Wool shop | 778 | Winchmore Sports Goods |
| W.T. Richardson, Estate agents | 780 | C. & H. Chinese Takeaway |
| Ernest Gilbert, Furriers | 782 | Curl Up & Dye Ladies Salon |
| Midland Bank | 784 | Midland Bank |
| Charles Ledsham Optician | 786 | Leslie Ricketts Estate agents |
| Leslie Ricketts, Estate agents | 788 | Leslie Ricketts Estate agents |
| Tottenham & District Gas Co. | 790 | David Way Furniture |

# INDEX

*The index refers to Chapters 1 to 9, and includes illustrations, printed in heavy type.*

207

209